A New Future

If, at any stage of reading this book, you feel inspi
read and want to speed up gaining useful insights 1
management and leadership skills, gain clarity on your situation, speed
up increasing your profitability, and build a firm you love working on,
then you are welcome to join The Law Firm Owners Club.

It's free, and as a member of this club, you'll get:

- A short email every other week with a core insight that you can
  implement right away to build an ever-more thriving and
  satisfying law firm.

- Free tickets to networking events I'll be speaking at; events where
  you will also gain further insights from other industry leaders.

- The opportunity to meet other law firm owners to share strategies
  to further speed up your profitability, reduce your heavy
  workload, gain free time, and do more of the work you enjoy.

If you'd like this or would like to find out more about possibly working
with Dan, go to:

www.danwarburton.com

Or scan this QR code:

Thank You!

Sofia, asking you to marry me was the best thing I ever did. I'm loving sharing this journey with you. I can't thank you enough for all the love and support you give me and our two (soon three!) wonderful girls.

Dad, you've no idea how much you've done for me. I wouldn't be at this level in my business if it weren't for you. You've shown me what it means to be ambitious and to never give up.

Mum, you are our amazing Nonna to our girls. You've always been amazing at keeping Dad and Chloe on the right path.

Chloe and Damian, my brother and sister, always supporting me and my ventures, however wild or impossible they may seem.

Chris and Scott (at Myerson Solicitors), you've no idea how much I appreciate all the wonderful clients you've introduced me to. I'm looking forward to continually succeeding alongside you both.

Simon Slater, thank you for all your amazing guidance and mentoring, which has enabled me to work with many inspiring law firm owners.

Francis Davis, thank you for taking the time to hear me speak and then taking on hosting my book launch event. It's an honour to work alongside you.

James Lumsden Cook, my amazing publisher. I love how you've shown me how to write more clearly and succinctly. It's only because of you that this book has not only been written to such a high standard but gained so many extraordinary testimonials.

Shaun Jardine, thanks so much for introducing me to your book publisher. It's only because of you that I am here, publishing this book.

Rob Hanna, thanks for being such a huge inspiration and showing us what it means to be truly revered in the legal sector. Also, thank you so much for writing the book's foreword. This is a great honour for me.

Michael Hinchliffe, thanks for all your amazing coaching and guidance in sales copywriting.

Build Big!

Delegate Now to Supercharge Your Profits

Dan Warburton

HAWKSMOOR
PUBLISHING

First published in 2025 by Hawksmoor Publishing

Woodside, Oakamoor, ST10 3AE

www.hawksmoorpublishing.com

ISBN: 978-1-914066-49-8

Hawksmoor Publishing has endeavoured to provide trademark information about all the companies and products mentioned in this book by the appropriate use of capitals. However, Hawksmoor Publishing cannot guarantee the accuracy of this information. Hawksmoor Publishing is an imprint of Bennion Kearny Limited. 6 Woodside, Churnet View Road, Oakamoor, ST10 3AE, United Kingdom.

Fiona Henderson, Grant Sanders, Maxine Heppenstall, Vikki Herbert, Tyrone Dutt, Adam Creasey, Ravie Govinder, and Patrick Gilmour, thanks so much for taking the time to read the first draft of the book and providing such extraordinary testimonials about its content.

To all my team that handles my marketing and admin, you operate quietly in the background, but I couldn't do all this without you.

To all of you who've had me speak at your event, hosted me on your podcast, or had me write for your audience, thank you so much. I wouldn't be here without you.

And to all my amazing clients, you know who you are. Thank you with all my heart for trusting me and letting me be part of your wonderful journeys to success.

Testimonials

I read Dan's book and found it insightful. It's a game-changer for law firm leaders. Dan clearly understands how law firms work, which made his suggestions and insights more relevant than any other generic business book. I have come away with a list of actionable points that will help me improve my management of our team members. As someone who finds it hard to have difficult conversations and hold someone else accountable, I found the concrete phrases he suggested and the structure to the conversations something I can take away and use for myself to help have those conversations in a positive way, rather than have them feel like an attack. Dan's deep understanding of law firm dynamics and actionable advice on delegation and accountability make this book an indispensable resource for any law professional looking to enhance their firm's profitability and get their leisure time back.

Fiona Henderson (Partner at Argyll Law)

———◆◆———

I am very lucky that during my career I have been provided with leadership training, so I was nodding along as I read Dan's book. Even so, I still gained some very useful insights. Often, lawyers are very bad at listening to their colleagues as they wait to speak and put their side across. This book made me reflect on how often I've done this myself. Now that I am conscious of it, this will further increase my ability to engage with my team effectively. In his book, Dan manages to distil what can be complex and sometimes challenging thoughts and ideas into simple and easily implementable actions. A must read for any law firm owner that feels they are not growing their firm as fast as they'd like to.

Grant Sanders (Partner at Stephen Rimmer LLP)

———◆◆———

As the MD of a midsize law firm, this book has made me clearly see that the power of listening and communication cannot be understated. A quick conversation across a desk is not enough; time must be specifically set aside. Also, I've learned that providing a safe space for people to speak their minds freely is vital to being aware of issues that need attention.

In his book, Dan uses his years of experience to guide you to see how you are being the 'bottleneck' in your firm's productivity, and it has shown me that profitable delegation and 'enabling others to effectively lead others' is the way forward. Without doing this, staff often 'quietly quit' as described in the book. This knowledge has allowed me to work with leaders in my firm in a much more effective way, spending time really listening to them and understanding what motivates them to come to work each day and motivate them to achieve their dreams. As a result of practising this, I have noticed that my team now invest greater time and effort in our firm.

Though a lot of this, I'd learned already from working with Dan over the last 12 months, which has been amazing, this book is a must-read for anyone involved in a leadership or management role. It sets out clear, achievable actions and objectives that will greatly impact any workplace.

Maxine Heppenstall (MD at Walker Foster Solicitors)

———◆◆━━

As someone with 20 years of experience as a practising lawyer in Corporate and Commercial Law, this book strikes a chord with the reality many of us law firm partners face daily in any jurisdiction around the globe.

Warburton's strategies provide a roadmap for law firm partners who feel exhausted from carrying out large volumes of billable work to streamline operations and lead effectively, ultimately creating more time to focus on our firm's growth while maintaining a healthy work-life balance.

One key insight I gained is the importance of profitable delegation, which means handing over tasks but ensuring that the delegation leads to high work standards, greater profitability, and freedom for the firm's leaders.

I'm also looking forward to implementing Dan's concepts around structured and strategic delegation in my practice, by training key team members to take over certain billable tasks and ensuring that workflows and technology support efficient operations, I'll have more time to mentor my team to grow the business while enjoying a balance between my professional and personal life.

For any law firm partner or leader who wants to elevate their firm's profitability while reclaiming precious time, this book is an indispensable resource. It encapsulates what it means to be a modern law firm leader—an entrepreneur who knows not only how to serve clients but also how to strategically build and manage a business that thrives.

Ravie Govender (Head of Corporate & Commercial at Cowan-Harper-Madikizela)

———◆·◆———

I found Dan's book really engaging and insightful. As I read it, I found it encouraging to know that other law firm partners like me have faced similar situations, and seeing how successful they have become is very encouraging. Seeing what is possible and learning some key strategies to lead and manage others has given me the confidence to take our firm to a whole new level, which you will want to do after reading this book, as Dan's encouragement and enthusiasm are infectious.

The book is written in plain language and is full of common sense, so the instructions are easy to apply to how we run our firms. I learned that it's key to be clear on our overall goal, how to be organised and structured with our communication, how to surround ourselves with the right people, and how to build a loyal workforce. All this, I know, will greatly speed up creating a profitable, happy work-life balance with happy employees. This book will be very useful for any law firm partner who is serious about succeeding.

Vikki Herbert (Partner & Head of Real Estate at Thackray Williams Solicitors)

———◆·◆———

I come from a family of entrepreneurs and have been doing business coaching for a while. Everything Dan said in his book makes so much sense to me, and it's confirmed that we're on track with what we're practising at our firm.

Whilst I may not be the best delegator or people manager, I am very familiar with everything Dan covered in this book, which, though it is not necessarily new to me, was great to crystalise everything I've already learned from starting my own law firm.

If only struggling law firm owners had access to such a book from the outset of their journey and the wisdom to implement what Dan covers, they would have enjoyed running their firm a lot more while being much more profitable in the short and long term.

This is a must-read for any law firm owner who feels they've hit a limit in their profits and are struggling to build a truly rewarding law firm with a positive culture."

Adam Creasey (Managing Director at Adam Benedict)

Though I'm an experienced law firm partner, I found investing my time to read Dan's book well worth it. The section about how to build loyal teams resonated with my findings, and I will make the most of the further insights I've gained.

I have been fortunate to be managed by idiots and by one extraordinary lawyer and delegator to feel the difference between being managed by others with good and bad people skills. However, feeling the difference and understanding the difference are two separate things and only by building my own department did I come to that understanding much later in life.

If I had read Dan's book when I first became a partner in a law firm, I think that law firm might still exist today. Instead, we were taken over by a firm which was ostensibly good at this stuff, and it took me another move and at least five more years to learn these lessons.

Dan has put some fundamental business-building lessons many law firm owners tend to avoid into a well-documented and easy-to-read form. It's a great book for any law firm owner who is wise enough to know they don't know it all.

Patrick Gilmour (Head of Corporate and Commercial at Anthony Gold Solicitors LLP)

<hr/>

As a law firm director, I found Dan's insights in the book practical and a refreshing departure from the usual management and leadership advice. What sets this book apart from other business and leadership books on the market is its focus on the legal profession and our unique challenges, especially in managing a team while maintaining profitability and balancing responsibilities outside the office.

This book brilliantly addresses the common pitfall that many of us law firm owners fall into – where we're stuck doing fee-earning tasks instead of leading and growing our firm. Dan offers a clear roadmap to creating a more profitable and sustainable business while reclaiming our time and energy to work 'on' our firm instead of 'in' it. Dan's examples are relevant and highlight the importance of learning to delegate profitably, not just delegating tasks.

In a market saturated with books on business efficiency and management, if you are a law firm owner looking to escape the trap of overwork and inefficiency, you are looking to take your practice and profits to the next level, *Delegate Now to Supercharge Your Profits* stands out as a must-read.

Tyrone Dutt (Director at Empire Law)

Table of Contents

Foreword

In today's legal world, running a law firm isn't just about providing excellent legal advice—it's about leading teams, optimising processes, and, most importantly, delegating effectively to drive profitability. Dan Warburton's book is an invaluable guide for law firm owners who want to step into the role of true leadership, moving beyond the day-to-day grind and into a place where they can focus on growth, strategy, and long-term success.

As someone who has worked closely with law firms across the globe, I know firsthand how difficult it is for leaders to strike the right balance between handling client work and managing their teams effectively. Dan tackles this challenge head-on, providing not just theory, but actionable steps that help lawyers shed inefficiencies, empower their teams, and ultimately boost their bottom line.

This book is not just about making more money—though it certainly provides the blueprint to do that—it's about reclaiming your time, developing a more engaged and motivated workforce, and unlocking your firm's true potential. Dan's insights are drawn from years of working with legal professionals, making them uniquely tailored to the intricacies of the legal world.

If you're a law firm owner or leader ready to take your firm to the next level, then this book is essential reading. Dan's wisdom will undoubtedly resonate with you, and I'm confident that by implementing his strategies, you'll see both immediate and long-term gains.

It's time to delegate smarter, not harder.

Rob Hanna, *Founder of KC Partners and Host of the Legally Speaking Podcast* ™

The Law Technicians
Valley of Doom

Over many years of working with law firm partners and owners to help them effectively grow their firm's profits (while achieving greater time freedom), I've identified one clear trap that most law firm partners fall into – indeed, *never* break free of.

It's a trap that can often only be noticed by someone looking from the outside in, by someone keenly studying a law firm owner's life and work routine.

In fact, I would go further. The observer needs to be someone who has already properly experienced owning or leading a business in the past. And by this, I mean someone who has built or led a business and then *experienced* it operating effectively and profitably whilst they only do a small amount of client work fulfilment, or even none.

Hold on, I'm going to go one step further. Not only must the observer have properly owned or led a profitable business, they must also have had the freedom to choose the hours they worked.

So, what exactly is the trap that I call *the law technician's valley of doom*? Let me explain through some examples.

Ronnie

Recently, I was contacted by the senior partner of a 50-person law firm based in the UK. Let's call him Ronnie. Ronnie's firm offered a broad range of legal services, including family law, conveyancing, probate, corporate law, and mergers and acquisitions. He reached out to me because he was hoping I could help.

Ronnie was in his early 50s and *exhausted*. He wanted to work fewer hours and not have to do heavy fee-earning work anymore; he no longer enjoyed it, and he'd been doing it for over 30 years. He also wanted to finally enjoy the success he'd gained from his life's work and spend more time with his family… but he couldn't. Even after more than 30 years of building his firm to a team of 50, he still had to do over 60 hours of work each week, with more than half of these hours being spent on billable corporate work.

This law firm partner was not free. He didn't own his law firm; his law firm owned him. It relied on him to keep operating. In turn, Ronnie no longer had the mental capacity or time to solve the many problems the firm was facing. These included a lack of effective marketing and sales, which meant the firm wasn't attracting new clients as regularly as it could. Furthermore, his teams' workflows were cumbersome and outdated, which meant Ronnie had to employ one admin operative per fee earner just to keep things moving, which was costly.

Ronnie also did not have time to check his employees' performance or distinguish what training they needed or who they needed to hire next. This meant that his team was not being utilised anywhere near as effectively as it could be. He also didn't have time to research and implement newly available technology solutions, so his outdated technology was further slowing down the performance of his team. All this was causing Ronnie's firm to miss out on a lot of extra profit and – ultimately – a lot of extra profit that he could pay himself.

Fundamentally, Ronnie didn't have much availability because he was so consumed with his fee-earning work. He had never learned how to profitably delegate away his workload, nor had time to train senior fee earners to take over the billable work he needed to do. As a result, Ronnie was stuck doing work he no longer enjoyed and was responsible for a law firm that was riddled with tiring inefficiencies. Worse still, he never had the time to solve these tiring inefficiencies.

So, the trap Ronnie had fallen into (and which many people like him also do) is plain to see. It's an inability to delegate effectively!

Valerie

Another partner I worked with recently (let's call her Valerie) was one of five partners in a 30-person firm. She was in her early 40s and wanted to work with me to learn how to effectively lead the 20 team members who reported to her. She wanted them to each bill more hours per month; Valerie understood how much more profitable this would make her firm.

The rest of the partners didn't want to delegate away their billable work because – even though most of them were exhausted, overworked and bottlenecks in the firm's productivity – they mistakenly believed that was the best route to the highest take-home profits.

The impact of this was that the non-partner fee earners didn't get much attention from Valerie. She was consistently focused on doing her billable work instead of getting the billing hours up for the rest of the team. This was causing her firm a major staff turnover problem as the non-partner fee earners weren't getting the training they wanted and chose to progress their careers elsewhere.

This was costing Valerie's firm a lot in recruitment fees and regularly left Valerie and the other partners stressed when handing off new staff and projects to clients. All this was very frustrating for Valerie because she *wanted* to take the firm to new levels of success. She was a young partner, but couldn't get the support she wanted from the senior partners – they also had little time for her due to their own billable work.

Valerie was caught in the classic legal profession trap.

Beatrice

I am sure you are seeing a pattern here, but let's have one final example.

Another law firm partner (let's call her Beatrice) that I consulted with recently was a lady in her late 40s. She was one of two partners in a 20-person firm and was exhausted from doing billable client work and managing her team. Beatrice was facing the additional problem that the only other partner in her firm was more senior than her and was retiring.

Beatrice's colleague, the older partner, had never learned how to delegate her workload effectively. Or, to put it differently, she hadn't effectively trained any of the other team members to take over the billable work she did. This was about to leave Beatrice in an even more overwhelming situation; she was about to become responsible for *all* her retiring partner's work on top of her own.

Stuck

Ronnie, Valerie and Beatrice were all stuck in this trap I'm referring to, the law technician's valley of doom. They were all under constant, heavy stress and could only see two options (selling their firms wasn't viable because they still relied on them far too much operationally).

The only two options they had were to either continue working exhaustively long hours (as they had done for many years to keep their firms running) or simply walk away from businesses they had worked so hard to build (losing everything). Neither Ronnie, Valerie or Beatrice could see a way out.

There is a way…

All the law firm partners and owners I've worked with were initially in a similar situation; they were all burned out from working long hours and couldn't see how to increase their firms' profits without working even longer hours.

They couldn't stop working, and they also could not take breaks to recharge their batteries very often. They took holidays infrequently because their firms relied on them so much to keep operating.

The solution that set my clients free of this trap, the law technician's valley of doom, was learning what I call *profitable delegation*. It's the skill that this book centres around.

> "
> It is literally true that you can succeed best and quickest by helping others to succeed.
> "
>
> **Napoleon Hill**

Note how I say 'profitable delegation' and not just 'delegation'. It's easy to delegate work away *ineffectively*: to have teams deliver terrible work, miss deadlines and operate half-heartedly. It's a very different skill to delegate work away and have it handled to a high standard whilst gaining a great reputation and making a firm reliably profitable.

Once a law firm owner masters how to profitably delegate their workload, doors open to new levels of financial and lifestyle success. Instead of primarily sitting at their desks – trying to hit their billing targets – they can focus on building and leading teams of 10, 50, 100 or more fee earners. Each of these individuals can focus on their own billing targets, whether these be fixed value-based or billable hours. Whatever the case, their firms will become more profitable than ever.

Maths

To fully understand this, let's do some simple maths.

As a law firm owner, if you bill yourself out at 500 (dollars or pounds or euros) per hour, that one hour of billable work (and you can't do anything else) will bring in 500 for your firm.

Alternatively, let's say your firm charges half of what you charge for an hour of billing completed by a middleweight associate. It's 250 (dollars or pounds or euros) an hour, and you have ten of these associates. In sum, when they all complete one hour of billing, they bring in a total of 2,500 of revenue.

Even once you factor out their wages and other staff costs, that one hour is still massively more profitable for you and your firm.

Now, if you multiply these numbers by ten – with 100 associates each billing instead of you – and even with the costs of, say, 20 back office support staff, it is self-evident that your measly one hour of billing is negligible in terms of the new profitability that you get to take home.

Until you understand how much more profitable your firm can be when your associates hit their targets (instead of you hitting your own billing targets), you'll always remain at your current level of success (or lack thereof).

If you enjoy doing some billable work, that's okay, but I suggest you keep it to low numbers so that your firm does not rely on you to be profitable. The message here is that you need to be free to truly and effectively lead and manage your firm's team members.

Profitable Delegation

Above all, profitable delegation is the key to a deeply fulfilling lifestyle for a law firm owner. Once implemented effectively, you can use the free time this creates to solve all the other problems your firm faces. These might include the implementation of new technology to streamline workflows, selling more services to existing clients, selling your services to new clients, marketing, attracting and retaining ideal new candidates, checking time recording, implementing solutions to keep up with compliance and regulations, plus any other challenge stopping your firm from achieving its profitability potential.

Not only this, but with profitable delegation, while your associates are billing, you can use your freed-up time to focus on *other* activities that matter to you. Maybe it is getting fit and healthy; maybe it is spending time with your loved ones.

This freed-up time can also be used to teach your senior members how they can profitably delegate away their workloads, which – in turn – increases their availability to manage their teams effectively. When their team members hit their targets, they create even more financial success for the entire firm, its owners, and you.

Law firm owners who don't learn how to profitably delegate away their workloads will one day have to face long and heavy hours whether they feel like it or not.

This is why the legal sector is renowned for mergers and acquisitions. At the end of a law firm owner's journey (one who is still relied upon for their firm to be profitable), there's no other choice but to sell the relationships they've built with their clients. Because this often doesn't work well, as they are the ones that are leaving, they can never get the money they deserve for all the hard work put into building their firm. Alternatively, they end up on a long, drawn-out, and low-paid employment scheme until they leave.

I'm not saying that learning profitable delegation is easy; it's not. It will take a serious commitment to becoming good at leading and managing others.

Are you willing to learn how to profitably delegate away your workload and free yourself from the law technician's valley of doom? Are you ready to step into an inspiring new future? Then let's begin!

> " The skill that enables a law firm owner to build a highly profitable firm, and be available to do their most enjoyable and important work is PROFITABLE DELEGATION. "
>
> **Dan Warburton**

Why Listen to Me?

There I was, in my mid-thirties, living in a tiny one-room bedsit apartment in Brighton, and things seemed to be going fine. I called myself *Super Dan the Handyman* and did everything off the back of a motorbike.

By this time, I'd completed many self-development programs that covered topics such as sales, marketing, entrepreneurship, leadership and management. Indeed, I was now in the second year of an intense two-year program on Team Management and Leadership, which was based on the principle that leadership isn't only about leading others to operate at a high level of performance, but that truly skilled leadership is about *enabling others to effectively lead others*.

The programs were incredibly demanding because we had to create projects that would genuinely make a positive impact on hundreds and even thousands of others' lives, and then hit handover deadlines where each project would be completely led and managed by a stranger! We also had to track complex statistics to *prove* the effectiveness of each project.

Not only this, but it was made clear to us that – even when under extreme pressure – manipulating or offering payment to anyone to be part of a project was never an option. Instead, we had to learn how to 'inspire' strangers to participate in our programs voluntarily. In turn, we had to find a way to leave everyone involved in each project feeling valued and respected.

It was at this point that I realised my handyman business only really succeeded through my personal hands-on hard work; my resources would always limit my level of success. In other words, there were only so many hours I could work in a day. If I were to build a truly successful business, one that could serve many people at once, I had to build a team to take over the handyman service I was delivering.

Within two years of gaining this new insight, I went from Super Dan the Handyman to the managing director of Team Super!

Team Super

We were a team of eight that offered a broad range of building repair services, from decorating, carpentry, gas works, and electrical work to plastering and some brickwork.

Through trial and error, I became more skilled at placing adverts in magazines, getting the phone ringing, writing out quotes, and closing sales. I also wrote out all the procedures for everyone to follow, from how to handle incoming calls, record client data, document the required work, deliver instructions to carry out each piece of work, track WIP (work in progress), carry out quality control checks, plus invoicing, and collections procedures. The times were good, so I kept saying yes to any building work that came my way.

At this stage, some of the workmen I'd contracted couldn't do the work they said they could, and began to make costly mistakes. I had to start paying other tradesmen from other companies to redo major pieces of work, which quickly used up more than my business profit. I knew business reputation was everything; I was determined to ensure every client was pleased with our work.

Because of the mistakes my workers were making, and because I couldn't lead the team to rectify each bad piece of work effectively, I hit a tipping point. I had clients wanting their work finished and workmen threatening me if I didn't pay their wages each Friday.

I was in a situation where I could either continue to pay myself a basic salary and not pay to have the bad work redone (thus gaining a bad reputation), or I could use my salary to rectify their bad workmanship. I chose the latter, took a major pay cut, and even loaded up on personal debt to pay for every bit of unsatisfactory workmanship to be redone properly and pay every workman.

The truth was I'd grown the business too fast. I'd employed workmen without long enough trial periods, and – most importantly of all – I hadn't *delegated* each project in a way that ensured the business would run profitably as a whole.

After four years of trading, I couldn't see how I could repay the debt I was in, and it was clear that we were no longer so super. I closed the business.

So, what went wrong? Firstly, the workmen just wanted their money and couldn't care less about the success of my business, and why should they? In turn, I hadn't communicated effectively what was in it for each of them. If they felt they were part of something great and were genuinely concerned about each client's satisfaction, they would have completed their work well and ensured every customer was pleased. If they didn't feel responsible for the success of the business as a whole, they'd always half-heartedly do their work and would be 'quietly quitting' (which is where the employees pretend to be busy but do the bare minimum work they can get away with).

Round two!

This time, I made things much simpler and chose to specialise by only offering 24-hour emergency plumbing and drainage services.

The idea came to me from speaking to others who were succeeding in this space. I learned that I didn't need to build a team from scratch; instead, I could just 'white label' someone else's team… so that's what I did.

I found a local plumbing business that was already set up, one that had a fair reputation and whose owner was interested in taking on more work. I then placed adverts in local magazines, spoke to customers on the phone personally, and closed each sale. Within six months, this collaboration was nicely profitable for me and for the contractor who collected payments and chased outstanding invoices.

Within a year and a half of launching this business, I was guiding the business owner, particularly on how to increase the reliability of his workforce. Here, we set up systems that tracked each workman's van location so he'd know who to action when new work came in.

I enjoyed not having to do any of the physical work or handle any of the team management. I could run the business completely remotely, and – because of the money I was earning – the freedom I experienced was extraordinary.

I ended up travelling to many places in Europe – including snowboarding in the Italian Alps and relaxing in luxury destinations on the Cote d'Azur – while the business ran with minimal input from me. I still had challenges, of course, such as dealing with disappointed clients when work was late, as they only wanted to deal with me. I had great visions for the company and was inspired to see if the model could be franchised. During this time, I continued to develop my professional education through courses and training.

At this stage, I was already a senior leader on one of London-based Landmark's leadership programs and was regularly guiding other ambitious participants. Because of the insights and results they gained, several would call me outside office hours to gain extra support. They would often tell me how our interactions had enabled them to break through the challenges – both professional and personal – that they had been facing. On top of that, I also had a number of neighbours, entrepreneurs, and other startup business owners ask me if I could help them build profitable businesses that would enable them to live fulfilling lives.

One day, I was having lunch with my father, my idol. He knew my career story (well, he's my father, right?) and surprised me by asking if we could have regular one-on-one sessions so that I could guide him on how to grow his business further. We did, and it was a success!

In January 2016, I told my father I was going to start my own one-on-one consulting business. Since then, this has been my only work focus, and I have now coached over 1,000 ambitious individuals (mostly made up of entrepreneurs and business owners).

Then, in 2020, I completed an advanced marketing program that was grounded in three main things.

1. Who our ideal client is

2. The problem we solve for them

3. What results we make possible for them (so we can communicate this clearly in our marketing)

From this, it was clear that the clients of mine that gained the greatest results – and whom I enjoyed working with the most – were law firm owners and partners, which is what brings us to this book. Over the last five years, I've chosen to work almost exclusively with law firm owners.

Law Firms

In the early days, one of my first law firm owners was Kim Nicol, a lawyer who provided workplace and employment law solutions. In 12 months, Kim went from being an unhealthy, overworked law firm owner to increasing her average monthly revenue by 310%. She gained an extra £192,041 in revenue in 12 months, employed her first team members, and reduced her work hours by 41%. She not only increased her profits but had the time to get fit and healthy.

Another project saw one law firm partner generate an 89% increase in his firm's profits (USD $707,794 extra profit) in less than six months while working half the previous hours.

Another went from working over 80 hours per week to less than 40, while taking her law firm's revenue from £13K per month to over £90K in less than a year.

Okay, I think you get the point!

Over time, I clearly saw that these stellar results stemmed from clients learning (and implementing) the advanced leadership and management skills I'd learned and – more to the point – the *delegation* strategies that I'd studied, implemented and refined over many years.

As I spent additional years interacting with law firm partners and owners, I realised why this work impacts their lives so effectively. It's because, for virtually all law firm owners, through your extensive academic training to become a qualified lawyer, or being an associate or owning a law firm, very few of you ever included training on how to effectively manage and lead teams of people.

Because of this, many law firm owners – even those with 100 employees – are likely to still feel overwhelmed when having to complete billable work alongside managing those who report to them.

This is because your large book of clients and billable hours got you promoted to partner level. And maybe, because of habit, focusing on billable work is more natural to you than stopping and delegating it to others.

One other thing I have noticed over the years of working with law firms is how much I have come to value and respect the work that lawyers do for society. Our world needs order and justice to protect everyone and our planet from greed-led destruction. Without you, our world would be in a much worse position than it is now.

I've also come to discover how underappreciated many lawyers are, how you work such long hours to protect people's homes, their belongings, their families, and the businesses they have spent so many years building. This is at odds, of course, with the resistance from certain clients not wanting to pay your firm for the heavy and skilled work you've done!

Now you understand *how* I've got to work with my law firm owner clients to achieve such results, let's get to work.

Vital Preparation

Before we get into the core Five Profitable Delegation Keys, I want to make sure you are ready for this.

The reason I say this is because what you are about to learn may – at times – feel awkward and challenging to implement. For this reason, you need a clear 'why' that motivates you to take effective action in the face of anything.

Your 'why' will be a mix of what you want and what you *do not* want. The clearer you become on the pain of what you *do not* want, the more you'll keep pushing through challenges as they arise.

Becoming clear-minded and feeling inspired by what you want will give you that extra motivation to keep going when things don't seem to be working as planned.

You've faced such times in the past, and you'll face more in the future. However, what I'm about to show you requires a bold commitment to not only implement, but to do so continually. It is this process of ongoing determination (for results to show up and to develop yourself in a rewarding and long-lasting way) that will pay truly rewarding dividends.

So, before you go any further, answer the following questions. Take your time and write them down. At a minimum, listen carefully to the answers in your head. Without a clear plan and direction of travel, how can you ever reach your destination?

Q. What will my life look like in 10 years if I keep doing what I'm doing?

Pause, re-read the question, and think.

Q. What will I likely never get to accomplish if I keep doing what I'm doing?

Again, pause, read this last question again, and think.

Q. Why do I want to learn how to profitably delegate away my workload?

Try to slow yourself down; don't rush this. Re-read this last question.

Q. What will become possible for me once I learn how to profitably delegate away the firm's workload, and I have lots of free time to focus on what matters to me?

Just think; imagine it.

Q. Who do I very much look forward to sharing my success with, and what difference will this make to their lives?

As I'm sure you've noticed, the last question isn't about you. This is because deep down – when you've got that dream house, the nice car, good health, and more holidays than you know what to do with – you'll be bored and will want something much deeper to keep motivating you. The one thing I've learned from all the self-development and business programs I've participated in is that nothing motivates us more than making a real impact in the world and getting recognised for doing so.

For now, spend time answering these questions and when you feel yourself getting angry with your current situation, feeling frustrated that your life isn't as you want it to be – while also feeling inspired by the things that will become possible for you, and the people that matter to you – then you are ready for what I'm about to show you.

If you don't gain this clarity, you likely won't have the motivation needed to achieve a truly long-lasting breakthrough in your levels of success.

Carlos Cruz-Abrams Case Study

In this interview with Carlos, we gain some deep insights into how, in six months, he went from exhaustion and working over 100 hours per week to under 50 – all while growing his law firm by five new members, creating time with his family, and enjoying regular skiing. At the same time, he gained USD $707,794.65 (GBP £596,734.00) extra profit, an 89.15% increase compared to the same six months of the year before.

At the time of this book's publication, Carlos is still the managing partner at CAS Law, which he calls a 'corporate transactional boutique'. The firm focuses on all aspects of corporate legal work for startup companies, venture capital firms, and private equity firms. It provides services such as corporate law and governance, contract writing, intellectual property due diligence, trademarks, and mergers and acquisitions in multiple sectors.

So, what did being a senior partner used to look like? What did he deal with?"

"I did everything. I worked a lot. I founded the firm six years ago, and we've grown incrementally over the last six years. When I met Dan, there were eight or nine of us.

"I worked all the time. Seven days a week. And I was doing all of the things necessary to run a business and grow a business. I was also helping to grow and foster other associates who were in the firm, while also doing business development, plus a lot of fee-earning work directly for clients. I was working probably about 100 hours a week.

"There was never a moment to take a breath, to appreciate what I had grown, appreciate the business. Instead, it was this constant scrabbling, having to work harder, having to work more, trying to catch up and trying to keep everything under control.

"There was no path toward enjoyment in what we were doing. It was literal survival for me."

Did Carlos know he had a problem and that there was some sort of imbalance?

"I think I knew I was working way too much, and I knew that it wasn't sustainable. We have fantastic clients who have a lot of work. And I think I knew that I needed to figure out some solution, but I wasn't sure what that solution was. I had no idea what it would even look like."

Carlos not only failed to research or find a solution for his exhausting situation, but he wasn't even searching for a solution because he didn't have the time to look.

"I was just struggling moment to moment, trying to keep our heads above the water. I mean, we were being very successful – it was going very well – but it was a lot of struggle for me personally."

At the time, Carlos had a satisfying take-home profit but was selling his lifetime to get it. And that was because he was doing a major part of the firm's billable work. A lot of people messaged him daily.

"Over 250 text messages a day," Carlos confirmed. "From my clients, from my staff, more importantly, from the people that I was working with, asking me questions. And it was a constant barrage of questions that everybody sent me in text."

Carlos found out about Dan from Yvonne Ribeiro, another client of Dan's.

"Yvonne and I are both consultants in a consortium of consultants that has brought together experts in different fields. Every month, I would come into our meetings – hair on fire – saying we've got to go quickly as I had so many calls lined up.

My thinking at the time was constant… I need to hire people! This was what I always said to myself and everyone. I need to hire people; I need to hire people. And then Yvonne sent me a message and said that there was someone I needed to meet, and that was Dan.

"Dan was very good at being separate and outside of our business, and able to look at things and help us digest our insights without trying to impose solutions. It really helped us to fathom where we needed to go.

"One of the first things Dan helped me to create, even on those initial calls before we were really working together, was a *goals list*. And he didn't ask me to do what I have always seen, which is breaking down where I wanted to be in a year."

Carlos thought about where he wanted to be in three years, before working backwards to one year and then to what he'd need to achieve in the next three months. Although the planning might appear back to front – starting off three years from today and envisaging the ideal lifestyle before getting clear on the milestones to make that vision a reality – it is a core part of Dan's methodology.

"Breaking things down into bite-sized, achievable things, to know where I want to be in three years, and what to do in the next week to move toward, was very useful. And I remember it was basically, 'How do you just get to work a lot less while greatly improving your personal take-home profits and the firm's take-home profits'."

Dan and Carlos had created an arrangement where he would work with both himself and his partner, Jenna, through weekly one-on-one and group calls.

"We talked about the text messages. Dan explained that I needed to tell everyone to stop texting me and only speak at agreed times each week. I did, and it cut from 250 to six text messages a day. I was like, 'Yes, this is the kind of help I need!'"

Dan, Carlos and Jenna also set and communicated boundaries about how they chose to be communicated with. This was a key factor that resulted in Carlos slashing the number of messages he received, but the key was putting structures in place that ensured everyone received adequate support to keep moving forward.

"We worked on the efficiency of communication. We talked about this a lot."

Carlos ensured that he learned to make clear requests, agree on deadlines, and hold team members to account in a direct manner.

"I have always tried to be the kind of leader who leads by example, which I still do. But in many ways, this meant prostrating myself for the benefit of others. If someone was too busy, I would do their work for them. So, I would think that if I showed someone I was too busy, maybe they would do something. But really, all it meant was that I did everything.

One of the main things we worked towards was no-fluff communication. How to make straight requests with people. How not to soften them to seem nicer. How do I avoid harsh feedback because I'm trying not to hurt someone's feelings? And it was really getting this idea of setting up regular communication with my team, which was important, like weekly calls with key members.

"Those weekly calls were – and continue to be – very work-orientated and focused in terms of the project they relate to. Asking them: Where does it stand? What does it need? What blockers do you have? Great, move forward on it. Okay, here's this deadline. Is this something you can achieve? No, what can you achieve? Okay, great, move forward on it.

"And it became this ability to have these very direct and clear communications so that I knew something was being done. People knew what was expected of them. And that created a much smoother and easier path forward in terms of having my team execute on work that I would just pick up and do if they were dropping the ball or – if done poorly – I would just fix and send on to the client.

"And now I am direct with my feedback, which is what wasn't working before. Some of the feedback I would get from my team was: 'Wow, I really love that; I know where I stand. I appreciate that feedback. I appreciate the very straightforward, no-nonsense feedback on this. I know what I need to do.

"Something I didn't realise was that people were hurt. If I was doing things they were supposed to do – and they didn't understand why I was doing them – people interpreted this as though I didn't trust them or didn't want them to do things. In actual fact, I really did want them to do things!"

Three months into working with Dan, Carlos had set up regular one-on-one calls with his partner-colleague, Jenna, and each head of department, plus a few middleweight team members to hold them accountable to agreed targets. He then reworked his firm's chain of command and placed each junior to only report to the middleweight members to reduce the number of one-on-one meetings Carlos had to lead. He also requested that the heads of department directly support those below them, also with regular one-on-one calls.

All this had a great effect on his team's efficiency; the firm's profits started to increase, and Carlos's workload decreased. This started to feel freeing for Carlos.

"In terms of fee earning, I have cut back significantly on the amount of fee earning that I do. What it has allowed me to do is earn fees from the very top, doing very heavy strategic work with clients. Now, I'm sending out the signature pages for everyone to sign. I've been able to cut back on all of those lower-level tasks. They still require skill and attention to detail, but they aren't the high-level strategic things that clients want to pay me to do.

"I've gone from billing 160 or more hours a month to 80 hours a month sometimes, which has improved my own quality of life as well as my ability to respond to clients and to help them. I now dive into the heavy strategic things they want help with."

So, what difference has this made to Carlos's lifestyle and the hours he works?

"I probably work about 50 hours a week now, so about 50% less than before. I think that's about right. To me, this was really important. I have a great family that I love very much, and one of my sons is going off to college next year. And I didn't want to miss this year with him. I felt like if I didn't change something, I was going to miss this year. And just being able to spend time with my kids more, being able to spend time with my wife, doing things that I love.

"I live in a beautiful place and I like to do outdoor things. And being able to do that and actually schedule those things into my life – such as skiing or biking – is just wonderful. The problem that I had before was that I was working more and living less. And now I'm able – most of the time – to find that balance."

But if Carlos is working less, surely he must be earning less now?

"I thought that as well, and I pushed against Dan for a long time as I am the highest billing person in our firm, and I bill at the highest rate, and I bill the most hours, so we're going to lose money. But one of the things Dan helped me work through was how we needed to grow our team.

"It wasn't efficient to have one person doing the work of three people, particularly in a business where you get paid for the time spent, because one person only has a limited number of hours. And, so, if you grow the firm, and you add three people, and you give the work of the one person who's very efficient (me) to three people who are possibly less efficient – still efficient, but not quite as efficient – together they can still get more work done.

"Now I have more time to bring in *more* work and feed it to more people. They can bill more hours. I review their work, which cuts down on my hours. I work with those clients, and our profits have gone up.

"I mean, we earned double, right? Our overall expenditure on expenses went significantly up. We spent $750,000 more on payroll and things like that because we grew the team hugely, and we feared that we were going to spend that money and see our profits go down because we're spending more. Our profits actually grew 34 or 40% year over year, *even with* that increase in expenditure. So not only did we spend that, but we also made the money to cover the expenditure.

"Plus, we made extra money on top of that. We looked at the last six months of last year versus the last six months of this year, which is the first six months Dan worked with me, and we saw that our firm had generated just over $700,000 extra *profit*."

Of course, that number did not take into account the commissions for Carlos, for business development, and law firm partner Jenna. Everybody's already been taken care of, so that number is true profit, right?

"Yeah, right. The key thing is it wasn't as though my salary was included in that profit number. That's in the expense numbers. That's really wonderful and has given us so much comfort in terms of seeing the path that we should continue to pursue.

"This growth path and this path of 'I don't have to do it all myself, but I can build a team that I can rely and trust on, who take the work and do the work and work with clients' – I can oversee that.

"Something important to Jenna and me is that we aren't doing a bait and switch with clients. We don't pitch ourselves and then pass them off to a team member. We do want to be involved with the client. We want to be involved with the work, but that doesn't mean we have to do every single thing."

What advice would Carlos give another law firm owner or partner about how to handle being the face of their firm and then having the team do the work instead?

"I think that it's a hard line, and I've seen some people be very successful at it and some people fail because there is this sense that – just because someone else is doing the work well – my hands are now tied. And it's absolutely *not* how I approach it now. It's absolutely *not* how Jenna approaches it either because we think that the buck still stops with you.

"The client still looks to you, so you need to know what's going on. You need to have a team that is keeping you in the loop, asking you questions, and who you can actually trust.

"Part of what we do in our regular meetings is to check in on every client and on everything that someone is working on every week... so there aren't surprises. And when the client calls me and says they are confused, I know what the client is talking about because I've had a check-in call with my team about it."

So, how do you find ideal candidates to join a firm in such a short period?

"We've used a lot of personal connections and have had incredible success building our team. In the last year, we went from eight when we started to 14 full-time people. That's six people that we added in just over six months."

One of the major problems Carlos had in his firm was the collections procedures because he didn't have the time to manage this properly. That was one of the things he wanted to have a breakthrough in because his firm was constantly owed so much for so long. The solution was clear.

"We hired someone who focused on just on collections."

Because Carlos was now working so much less and had more time, he could allocate time for specific training to solve specific breakdowns across his firm. This included training the collections team to collect effectively. This enabled Carlos to manage key team members, who were then able to collect a lot of the money that the firm was owed.

"That was one of the key things we had to develop, our own systems for ourselves and our practice; firm-wide systems that I did not have time to develop before. Sometimes, I still feel like I don't have time, but that's the nature of being a law firm partner. And I understand that working 50 hours a week is more than most people work at their jobs, but going from 100 to 50 feels really nice."

What does Carlos look forward to?

"I talked about this yesterday. Kaizen. The concept of never-ending improvement. There are a lot of things that I have taken onboard in the last six months, and I have learned and had personal breakthroughs in my communication. I've also recognised where I have weaknesses and how I can work on them. I want to start implementing this with my team more, and I look forward to understanding, frankly, how to train my team in many of the ways that Dan trained me.

"I think that efficiency is what I try to strive for every single day; I want my team to try to strive for it in their own jobs. I think that it's essential to recognise that your team, as you grow and build them, are not just drudgery workers. I mean, these are people who are trying to build careers. These are potential partners down the line. These are people who are hoping to do what I do.

"So, I want to mentor them, and I want to help them develop and grow into the lawyers and businesspeople they want to be. And the way for me to do that is to help them start to implement what I've been trying to implement. Because, frankly, if we're all shooting on all cylinders, imagine what we could do, right?

"I mean, we can see in the next six months that I will be able to further delegate my work away than I am currently, reduce my fee-earning work more, focus more on business development and probably hire another one, maybe even two fee earners.

"I still have discomfort when I cut back on my fee-earning work. I don't want to stop doing fee-earning work; I want to do the *really important* fee-earning work, right? I really want to do value-added fee-earning work for the clients because they pay a lot per hour for me to do that work. And, so, I want to make sure that I'm focusing on that highest and best use of fee-earning time, and not wasting fee-earning time."

Carlos demonstrates, above, how much more efficient and profitable his firm is when he delegates the lower-level fee-earning work he used to do. This enables him to build his firm effectively with freed-up time.

"I think that adding more people will allow that further refinement and cover for the fee-earning work that I do. I'll have more time and further ability to go out and get more business, which will bring in more work and grow the work that our team has to do. This is just going to continue to grow our profit."

So, would Carlos like to get down to 40 hours a week?

"That would be wonderful. That's one of our three-year goals, but we're going to do it in the next six months. Part of what I'm really interested in is trying to get my work down to what I would call normal people levels. And I would like to spend even more time with my family and, you know, even more time doing the things I love."

Carlos explains how he thought that he could either have time for himself and his family *or* his work, but now, this isn't the case.

"Before, it was always a trade-off. I could spend more time with my family, which meant that I would spend less time doing work, earn less money, and be less successful on the work side. Or I could spend more time trying to grow the business, grow the work, grow all that stuff, and

I would have to ignore my family; ignore those things I like to do in my life.

"I've seen it doesn't have to be a trade-off. If you have the right processes, the right team, and the right, no-fluff communication, you can spend more time doing the things you love while successfully building your business. Not killing yourself and still growing your profit.

"And I think it's hard for others to picture. And it's just not true; there's no magic, there's nothing special about me that allows me to be able to focus on my family, life, and build a successful business without sacrificing one for the other. It's that there are tools, particularly as lawyers, that we were never taught. Efficiency is not a lawyer tool. Frankly, efficiency is something that is not rewarded when you're working in a big law firm."

What is meant by efficiency?

"Developing systems in which work can be done more quickly, or where more team members can do work more efficiently. It might earn a lower fee on an hourly basis if done by other team members than if I did that work, but if we can spread work among many team members – overall – the pie just becomes bigger.

"I think what I keep coming back to is if I bill at 1 X and someone else bills at 0.5 X and someone else bills at 0.5 X and someone else bills at 0.5 X, but I'm the only one doing the work, I'm missing out on an extra 0.5 X. If I don't have three other people doing all of this work instead of me, I'm missing out.

"And if they're doing a lot more billing, then I'm able to focus on business and team growing and client growing and all of those things. Before, I was making sacrifices when I thought I was growing the business but I was actually hurting the business. And that's a perspective that it took a while to realise; all of these things that I thought were necessary to grow the business further were holding the business back.

"Dan's approach works for any law firm owner. I think that a lot of people probably think that it's for a small firm, and yet even mine, which is middling, benefited greatly. I also recently told someone how this would work well for partners at big law firms because they're trying to figure out how to find their niche within a larger law firm. How do I manage a team? How am I building my business? Anyone can benefit from this.

"I would say, take a moment to look at what your biggest pressure or suffering points are. Think about what seems absolutely intractable to you. What are the things that you say, 'This is there, but it's unchangeable; there's nothing I can ever do about it?' Because those are the things where I discovered something new.

"What's amazing to me is that we have been able to continue to build our culture while hiring really effective team members and maintaining that culture. Before, we were so focused only on culture – and not effectiveness – that we were driving ineffectiveness. And, then, the only thing that was driving culture was me and my partner… again, killing ourselves by trying to do so much fee-earning work."

So, what does Carlos conclude?

"You don't have to necessarily give up. I had reached a point where I'd been doing this for over 20 years, and I thought, 'Okay, I can just stop. I'll do something else, because I'm tired of it. And this is hard. And it's been hard for 20 years. And it's not something I enjoy. And I'm never going to enjoy it.' And I think that the answer is, again, we as lawyers are trained to look at other people's problems and find real-life practical solutions for those problems. And we often forget to look at our own.

"Lawyers are notoriously bad at asking for help. Instead, take that first step, actually have the conversation. Worst case scenario, you end up exactly where you are today.

"I think many business owners, law firm owners, think it'd be nice to have somebody else to do the work. But if somebody else does the work, we never get to grow; we never get to learn; we never get to master all those leadership skills. And the only way of mastering those leadership skills is to face what's stopping us from owning our greatness and taking those actions that matter. I've probably grown more in the past six months, personally, and work-wise, just because of the work I've done together with Dan."

The 5 Profitable Delegation Keys

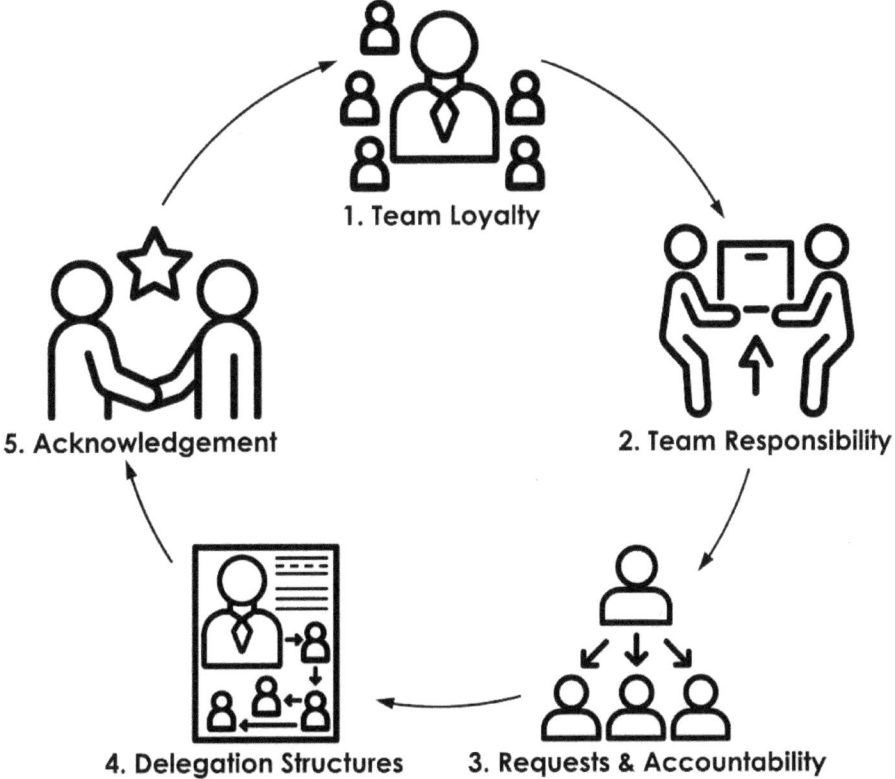

1. Team Loyalty

2. Team Responsibility

3. Requests & Accountability

4. Delegation Structures

5. Acknowledgement

Now that you've read Carlos's story, and what learning the art of profitable delegation made possible for him, we'll get to work on the formula this book centres around: the 5 Profitable Delegation Keys. Above is the formula. The keys are ordered most effectively with regard to their implementation, but the magic truly happens when all 5 keys become part of your and your firm's members' daily practice.

1. Team Loyalty

How many clients can you provide extraordinary service to when *you* are the one doing the work? You may be able to have several clients' pieces of work underway at once, but you can only work on one piece of work at a time. You can't write out two documents at once, you can't speak to two clients at the same time, and you can't be in two places at once.

The larger your firm's team is, the greater the number of clients' you and your law firm can impact at once, but the larger your team, the more challenging they are to manage at high performance levels.

> **"** Great things in business are never done by one person; they're done by a team of people. **"**
>
> **Steve Jobs**

Because of the leadership and management challenges involved with running larger teams, the larger the team, the lower the level of service each fee-earner can usually provide to each of your clients.

The volume of work that your firm can do will be relative to the number of team members in your firm. It is self-evident that the more (manageable) team members in your firm, the more work your firm can process at once, and the more profitable your firm can be.

Regardless of the number of team members in your firm, for them to perform at least relatively effectively, they must demonstrate a decent level of loyalty to you. They must effectively support you to ensure your firm continues to succeed.

That support involves moving towards agreed targets relatively well, and in a way that's based on everyone upholding values such as honesty, compassion, and respect.

When team members don't feel loyal to you or the success of the firm, it's probably because they don't feel they are getting what they want from their position in the company. As a result of this, you'll likely experience team members breaking their contracts and leaving their employment positions early.

As Liz Smith, a highly in-demand headhunter who specialises in attracting and moving top talent in law firms, wrote on LinkedIn recently:

I'll cover one of the most common reasons why I manage to move senior associates when they're NOT LOOKING TO MOVE and NOT UNHAPPY in their role.

Transparency.

Lawyers like to know stuff. They like to feel in control of their work, their lives, AND their careers.

But so many firms don't offer a transparent career path and because of this, I can attract a 'settled' senior associate and move them into the Partner role THEY'RE READY FOR or a role which offers a well-defined, documented path to partnership within a timeframe.

Firms which offer clearly thought-out career frameworks, underpinned by core values, behaviours and leadership qualities which work towards the strategic direction of the firm, benefit greatly from staff retention. It provides lawyers with a roadmap for professional growth.

Lawyers can see a future with their firm. They understand key skills they need to develop and objectives that need to be achieved, AND they can learn from lawyers ahead of them who deliver on this and get promoted.

The law firm owners earning truly satisfying levels of profit – while having the free time to focus on what matters to them – are supported by a team of loyal people.

With this in mind, if you want to build a highly profitable law firm and one that gives you the free time to focus on what matters to you, you must build a team that's loyal to supporting you in succeeding to build a great business.

Loyalty

So, how do you lead your team in a way that makes them loyal to you?

The Oxford Dictionary defines 'Loyalty' as:

1. The quality of being loyal. Giving the example of, "His extreme loyalty to the Crown."

   and:

2. A strong feeling of support or allegiance.

It makes sense that if your team are not loyal to you – helping you achieve your vision and hitting your firm's financial targets – they'll not only hold you back but collectively operate at painfully low levels of performance, too.

Like a crew in a rowing boat, if some team members aren't rowing at all or worse still are rowing in a different direction, it will be down to the few committed crew members to row correctly, which is very destructive to overall team performance.

When everyone in a rowing crew rows the boat in the same direction and in a well-synchronised manner, by contrast, the crew operates at a high level of performance, and the boat moves in the right direction effectively and with speed.

So, a truly thriving law firm requires loyal team members. Firstly, you need to establish whether your team members are loyal (or not) and support you in achieving targets.

Do your team members do any of these things?

1.   They turn up late for meetings with you.

2.   In group meetings, they don't participate by giving suggestions.

3.   They often call in, saying they are unwell and want to take the day off.

4.   They don't do what you ask of them.

5.   They don't hit deadlines.

If you are experiencing any of these things from your team members, then they are not demonstrating loyalty.

Valerie

When Valerie (not her real name), an owner and founder of a conveyancing firm, came to me in early 2023, she was experiencing all of these five points.

She was exhausted and felt that she had to do everything in her firm, from ensuring the firm's clients were pleased with the work, to doing a lot of billable work herself, and (worst of all) redoing client work and finishing it herself before releasing it to the client.

We then worked together for a year, and by the end of it, Valerie had not only managed to delegate away all the billable work she would normally do (thus freeing up her time), but her firm increased its revenue over 10-fold.

What made this possible was initially making the tough decision to end some team members' employment contracts, and then recruiting and employing new team members based on absolute clarity on the roles she wanted each person to fill.

Valerie then learned how to lead her team in a way that made them loyal to supporting her, loyal to the firm's clients, and most importantly able to hit their billing targets – completing work to a high standard so it could be delivered directly to clients.

Most of my clients have experienced great upticks in the performance and profitability of their firms once team members begin to demonstrate loyalty in supporting them.

Three Points

Garnering loyalty is not rocket science. Through many years of leadership training, and more than five years of hands-on practice with law firm owners, these three main points shine through consistently.

1. Listen fully. Leave whoever is speaking feeling heard and respected.

2. Conduct regular one-on-one conversations with team members, especially those who manage others below them.

3. Do *what* you say you will do, and by *when* you have agreed to do it.

Let's start with number one – listening. Listening is the most vital skill any leader needs to practise if they are to inspire or motivate those around them and generate loyalty.

Listening

Listening really is the most undervalued skill when it comes to leadership and – when in conversation – it is not trying to be right or prove a point. It's not trying to work out what to say next to impress.

Listening is not waiting for your turn in a conversation, so you can then express your opinion and try to 'win' the discussion. Listening is also not happening if you let yourself drift off into a daydream about something while someone is speaking to you.

Listening is:

1. Aiming to leave whoever is speaking feeling heard and respected.

2. Being more interested in leaving team members feeling important (rather than impressing them).

3. Being interested in seeing how you can help.

4. Being so 'present', when in conversation, that all your other concerns disappear.

5. Replying in a way that clearly demonstrates you were listening.

These steps can prove most difficult during a heated discussion and when points of view about how to handle something are very different. Even in these moments, the art is to ensure that whoever speaks to you is certain you 'get' their experience, and that you empathise with their viewpoint (even if it seems ridiculous) *before* offering a suggestion or a solution.

If you don't ensure someone who feels frustrated or angry 'gets' that you acknowledge their feelings, or the situation they are in, before responding, it usually doesn't matter what you say – it will likely be ignored.

I'd like you to think of the last conversation you had with one of your firm's fee earners or heads of department, and reflect on the five points above. Then, ask yourself for each: *did I practise this?*

If you didn't, then this is the gap for you to close.

If you practise listening fully when conversing with your team members, and practise each of the five points above, you will quickly deepen your relationship and level of connection with each team member.

Subsequently, this becomes a solid foundation for the relationship you have with each colleague that you can build from; a foundation that will cause each team member of yours to feel like reciprocating by listening more intently to *your* views and requests.

In turn, each team member will start to demonstrate a deeper level of care towards doing what you ask of them, and care towards client needs.

One-on-One

Let's break down the second of our three principles for generating loyalty… having regular one-on-one conversations with key team members.

No one will ever want to be loyal in striving for your firm's objectives if they don't feel that there's something in it for them; this is human nature.

Money is only *part* of the equation. Today, many of the younger generation(s) value well-being and the time they get to spend with family and friends more highly than the size of their paycheck, so motivating those who feel this way with a pay rise will usually be ineffective.

In 2014, the academic Dan Stone published an article on his website entitled: "What is a Functional Relationship to Money and

Possessions?" He went on to explain in depth how people are often motivated by the functions or the activities that money makes possible, rather than the money itself, writing: "A functional relationship to money is nonmaterialist, financial resources are merely a means to achieving nonfinancial, transcendent goals."

But what if an employee of yours doesn't know what their nonfinancial and transcendent goals are? In this case, they will like the sound of 'more money' but won't have the motivation to work towards earning more money by stretching themselves (especially if they don't know 'why' they are employed within your firm).

There will, of course, always be a handful of employees who will never know what they want. They will settle for employment just to be paid a reasonable salary and won't strive for more.

If such employees deliver a good standard of work (and on time), then they are still a great asset to your firm, and you simply need to do what you can to ensure they don't leave! This will likely involve them feeling respected and valued by you, alongside their regular payments for services rendered.

Other associates will be more motivated by gaining status, feeling part of something, getting to impact others' lives in a meaningful way, or being able to bring stability to their loved ones. And, for others still, it might be about career progression and becoming a partner alongside you. The take-home here is that what motivates each employee will be varied and the only way you'll discover people's motivations is by *asking them*.

What I'm proposing here is that you let go of merely being your employee's boss (who pays them money for work in return) and instead also become their mentor.

Becoming a mentor demonstrates patience in helping a staff member work out what they want. Then, help them to accomplish their ambitions by meeting targets you set for them.

> **"** The most important thing in communication is to hear what isn't being said. **"**
>
> **Peter Drucker**

Why?

You might be thinking, 'Why is it the partner's responsibility to give associates what they want to entice them to stay?'

Well, if you don't, it is likely that disenchanted employees will break their employment contracts early, and you'll have to face painfully high recruiting fees to replace them. Often, you will also have to use a lot of resources to train their replacements.

On the other hand, if you become the mentor to your employees – or certainly to at least five to ten key team members under you – and you genuinely guide them to ensure they succeed at what matters to them, doesn't it make sense that they will show you loyalty? Doesn't it make sense that when you request them to do something for you, they will be willing to help and that this will increase the profitability of your firm?

The key point here is listening fully to your key employees, managers, or heads of department in one-on-one meetings, then asking questions such as:

- Why are you at this firm?
- What would you love to succeed at?
- If anything could become possible through your employment here, what would you love that to be?

Then it's about leaving team members feeling like they can never say anything wrong to you; that you've got their backs and that you want them to succeed at what matters to them.

To be clear, motivating and inspiring people to be loyal to you and your firm will never happen with only emails and texts.

It can only happen when a major part of the communication between you and your key team members is in verbal conversation, and you operate not only as their employer but also as their mentor.

Practising this will get the greatest performance possible out of each employee.

Once your team members get that their one-on-one conversations with you are to ensure their success, they will become much more loyal.

We will cover more of this in Chapter 3, Delegation Structures.

Deliver!

Now, onto our final principle: doing what you said you'd do, and by when you said you'd do it.

It makes sense that if you arrange a time to meet a team member, and you turn up late or not at all, this employee won't feel respected or valued by you on some level.

If you continue to do this, and they don't feel valued by you, they will feel much less motivated to perform at a good level towards helping you achieve your and your firm's targets.

In turn, being late or missing appointments with your clients, not just your employees, promotes more of this behaviour in your team. You make it seem acceptable to behave this way.

Then, when you request your team members to do something, and you agree on a time frame for them to complete the task you've requested, it is highly likely they will follow suit and let you down by breaking deadlines. They will have begun to lose (or never gain) the understanding of how important it is to be true to their word. Why would they if the boss doesn't?

As a leader, you need to fully walk the talk. If, for example, you say that you stand for equality but never employ anyone from a minority background, or that you stand for a charitable cause but never donate to that cause, or that you value everyone being respectful towards each other in your firm but you often shout and lose your temper with your staff, you won't gain trust and loyalty from your team members!

Fundamentally, employees failing to display trust towards you is often caused by you not 'behaving' as you speak; for people to feel loyal towards you, it's vital that they trust you first.

Not being true to your word causes a visible disparity between what someone hears you say and what you do, which – in turn – breaks down their trust in you. It's then very difficult to inspire your team members to be loyal to you and your firm's business objectives.

So, when it comes to building a team that is loyal, you *must* get the importance of being true to your word. If you set an appointment or agree to do something for someone (anyone), do whatever it takes to be on time; if you are going to be late, even by one minute, send a text message to let them know.

If you want team members in your firm to practise good values such as respect, kindness or honesty, display them *yourself* in every moment and every situation. If you ever fail to do this, get into conversation with those around you and highlight the disparity between what you've been saying and doing. Make a renewed promise to behave as you say.

Team Loyalty Revision

- Practise fully listening and leaving whoever you are speaking with feeling heard and respected. Do this *before* trying to move a conversation forward, especially when in heated conversations.

- Hold regular one-on-one conversations with your key team members. Request that they do the same with each of their team members.

- Do what you say you will do. Do it when you say you will. If you break your word, take responsibility for it and propose what you will do differently going forward so it doesn't happen again.

- To gain truly great loyalty from your firm members, line managers must be aware of what they want to accomplish. They must be supported in achieving this as a by-product of *their* success at your firm.

2. Team Responsibility

One big problem that law firm owners face is trying to lead a firm with a blame culture.

This kind of work culture can often go unnoticed by business owners because it's so common and seen as normal. On the occasions when law firm owners do notice it's going on, it seems like a problem that is too big to solve; they sweep their awareness of it under the carpet and continue with business as usual. But this lack of awareness greatly decreases their ability to build a great law firm.

> " The secret is to gang up on the problem, rather than each other. "
>
> **Thomas Stallkamp**

The main cause of a blame culture is company values that lack responsibility. This sees teams made up of people who often avoid taking responsibility for their lack of performance and mistakes; instead, they tend to blame others, creating a vicious cycle of more blaming.

This bad culture is kept alive in your firm by team members blaming:

1. You
2. Clients
3. Their colleagues
4. Having too much work to do
5. The firm's procedures
6. Not being able to find a document
7. Not receiving an email
8. Technology

9. Weather

10. Anything they can think of!

Above all, a blame culture develops and is kept alive across teams when the leaders blame their team members or destructively criticise them for their lack of performance or when they make mistakes.

A blame culture is also fuelled by leaders who never hold their team members to account and who let them perform at low levels of performance before stepping in to redo client work or complete it themselves before submission.

> **"** A leader's job is not to do the work for others. It's to help others figure out how to do it themselves, to get things done, and to succeed beyond what they thought possible. **"**
>
> **Simon Sinek**

In doing so – over time – employees and associates become reliant on the firm leaders and become accustomed to not taking responsibility for completing their work. Because of this, they don't practise taking responsibility; in the absence of taking responsibility, blaming is easily adopted.

A blame culture has a devastating effect on business and team performance because the cause of bad performance is continually being hidden by the perpetrators. This is because the perpetrators don't want to get caught or be held accountable for their bad performances or mistakes.

Clifford Frank

When my client, Dr Clifford Frank, came to me in mid-2023, he'd spent many years building his law firm but had a team that frequently left him frustrated as they could never hit their monthly billing targets.

This meant that Dr Frank continually had to be one of the main fee earners in the business to ensure his clients were kept pleased and to maintain the turnover his firm had at the time.

Because of this, he never had time to solve the wider problems, including outdated IT and technology. He also felt his firm couldn't take on more work as he couldn't rely on his team to get the work done. It is self-evident that his firm's profits were limited as a consequence.

Soon after we started to work together, one of the tasks Dr Frank undertook was to speak with his associates to find out why their hours of billing were so low.

We then discovered it was because they weren't recording their time! So, we dug deeper to find out why they weren't recording their hours fully.

Virtually all of them blamed their workflow management software locking them out, the technology being slow, and not being able to access client data. Some said they didn't even know of the billing targets they needed to meet.

Though some of these claims might have been true, everything they said was to avoid being held responsible. They blamed everything else around them instead of *taking responsibility* for their lack of performance and offering to *solve* what was stopping them from completing enough billable work or recording their hours effectively.

Once Dr Frank became aware of this, he put in place easy-to-use time-capturing systems and procedures so he could track each associate's performance regularly.

Soon after, he could demonstrate to each associate the billable hours they were each recording, and show which associates were still not hitting their agreed billing targets.

At this stage, they were no longer able to blame the time recording systems, and as a result, Dr Frank was able to calculate the profitability of each associate. In doing so, we became aware of which employee to invest in (and keep in the firm) and who to let go of. However, the main takeaway here is that it took Dr Frank eliminating what they were blaming to determine how reliable each team member was.

Of course, even after implementing such new structures in a firm, if a culture of blame permeates the company, employees will always find something new to blame for their lack of performance. As such, it's vital that if a blame culture is present in your firm, you start to lead team members in a new way that inspires them to stop doing this.

History Repeating

When people in a firm continually blame conditions outside of themselves, your problems with those employees will repeat, and low performance will continue.

A blame culture makes it difficult to discover if team members need to grow and develop skills, so they often don't get the training they need. If growth and development are slow, these people often become a dead weight that slows the rest of the team down.

One of the main causes for team members habitually blaming conditions is a *fear* of expressing themselves fully; a *fear* of speaking out about what challenges they face. In essence, they are scared of 'looking bad' in front of their bosses and colleagues.

They then avoid asking for the support they need, continue to operate at a limited level of performance, and continue to blame you, your firm's technology, and anything else they can think of!

The opposite of a 'blame culture' is what I call a 'responsibility culture', and this is a thriving environment that feels amazing for everyone to work in.

I've observed that the highest-performing law firms have a team of individuals who reliably *take responsibility* for the quantity and quality of their work output. Team members who feel responsible for ensuring the firm's clients have their needs met.

With team members who feel this way and who behave responsibly towards the law firm's clients, owners find it much easier to delegate away their firm's billable work.

Generating 'Responsibility Culture'

So, how do you move a firm's culture from blame to taking responsibility?

Here are the three core practices required:

1. Always look for what *you* can take responsibility for first (even when others make mistakes).

2. When you don't complete something well, or by when you said you would, don't hide it. Clear it up in a conversation!

3. Stop speaking badly about someone else behind their back. Campaign a company-wide policy to stop others from doing so.

Let's expand on point 1, always be looking for what you can take responsibility for. When we feel let down – when someone doesn't do their work well or when they don't deliver on time – it can be easy to get frustrated and feel angry towards them. Yet, it is *especially in these moments* when we must be compassionate towards whoever has underperformed.

If we don't do this, and we aggressively challenge whoever has let us down in an angry voice and make angry gestures towards them, it only makes them want to hide future mistakes from us even more. They will seek to further avoid having to speak to us, and avoid telling us what challenges they face. Fundamentally, they will find that blaming others, you, and external circumstances for their lack of performance is their only option.

If you were to continue being frustrated and angry with colleagues, soon enough many – if not most of them – will start to talk badly about you behind your back.

Not only this but if you ever wanted their opinion about how to improve something in your firm (e.g., marketing, workflows, time recording processes, etc.), many will fear speaking their mind. It becomes inevitable that they will only say whatever they think you want to hear. This will leave you with a false idea of what to focus your energy on next.

Anger

Do you sometimes or often demonstrate anger towards your associates, employees, or co-partners?

If so, then the first thing you must pledge is to practise never doing so again. This may sound easier said than done, so the key word here is practice.

What you continually practise, you improve. Courageously take responsibility for *your* ineffective communication, and make a vow to start practising effective communication at all times – from now onwards – with everyone.

> " To effectively communicate, we must realize that we are all different in the way we perceive the world and use this understanding as a guide to our communication with others. "
>
> **Tony Robbins**

If you hold yourself back and don't give in to the urge to express your anger and frustration towards your employees and colleagues in an uncontrolled way, you will notice that you will get better over time at handling those intense feelings, even if they never go away.

You are human.

At times, you will have intense negative feelings but the skill here – the way you'll move your team from habitually blaming to taking responsibility – starts with *you* practising not expressing *your* frustration and anger towards your employees. A simple technique to reduce angry outbursts is deliberate breathing. Spend ten seconds breathing deeply in moments when anger surfaces, until the intense feelings subside. In a calmer frame of mind, ask yourself:

What can I take responsibility for in their mistake or their lack of performance?

Unhelpful Thoughts

As I write this, you might be thinking a couple of things…

Firstly, why should I take responsibility for my employees not doing their work effectively when I'm paying them?

If this is happening, it might signal a tendency to blame (instead of taking responsibility for) the performance your employees operate at.

If you continue to think and *behave* this way, you'll only promote a mentality of responsibility avoidance. The only way you can nurture your firm's culture is by leading from the front, by courageously taking responsibility for all the ineffectiveness and breakdowns in performance you are experiencing – both in yourself and in your firm.

Doing so is challenging initially, but soon becomes very rewarding because you move yourself from being someone who blames to someone who facilitates change. In this, you become a detective, someone less affected by others' lack of performance, and someone who solves problems and moves forward in new and effective ways quickly.

Even more importantly, you will start to *inspire* your employees, associates, and partners to behave in the same way. You will see them taking responsibility and rejecting blame, for not only their lack of performance but for those around them.

Take note that taking responsibility doesn't mean you get angry with yourself when someone doesn't do something well. The art, here, is to let go of blaming everyone and yourself altogether.

To help with this, I offer the following statement as a guide. Many of my clients have found it profoundly effective when practised. When they first heard it, many of them wrote it down on a sticky note and pinned it to the edge of their computer screen.

There is never anything wrong, there is only ever something missing.

There is Never
Anything Wrong

There is Only Ever
Something Missing

Carlos

When Carlos, the senior of two law firm partners of a 10-member law firm, joined one of my programs, he was exhausted from working over 100 hours per week.

For a lot of this time, he used to carry out billing work and complete or redo work that wasn't finished or not completed well by his team members.

In an attempt to create and maintain a great culture across his firm, Carlos and his co-partner would avoid holding their team members to account because they didn't want to upset anyone by being too demanding of them.

They were paying their employees and associates well, so – naturally – they were frustrated with the lack of performance their team gave back.

Up to this stage, Carlos thought that showing his team members how he was so busy and overloaded with work would cause them to step up their efforts and help him more, but this never happened.

Because of this, Carlos built a firm that had a great culture (the team members were kind to each other, and everyone enjoyed a good work-life balance), but the *responsibility* to complete most of the work to a good standard often fell back on Carlos and the other partner.

Because of this, Carlos often found himself blaming his team members for not working effectively. He typically had to deal with over 250 messages a day from team members needing advice or questions answered.

Once Carlos started seeing the truth in the statement 'There is never anything wrong, there is only ever something missing', he was able to let go of blaming his team members and start to ask:

What can I take responsibility for in the performance of my team members?

During one-on-one video calls with me, Carlos distinguished that his employees kept messaging him because he made himself available to them at all times, and he kept giving them the answers. He kept putting himself in a place where he was relied upon by the rest of his team in order for his firm to continue operating and being profitable.

Once Carlos was no longer blaming them, he was able to take responsibility for their lack of performance. He did this by getting into conversations with each of his fee earners and saying sorry for not giving them what they needed to hit their billing targets.

From there, he requested that team members no longer message him (unless necessary, of course) and that each key employee took their questions to him in a weekly one-on-one call.

He then used these regular one-on-one calls to elevate each fee earner's performance by training them, making clear requests of them, and holding them to account on agreed targets. This, in turn, led to the empowerment of his team.

Carlos was able to do this and not let frustration trigger him back into doing the work himself by always remembering that *there is never anything wrong and that there is only ever something missing.*

By learning this, he is now able to stay in effective communication with each of his team members, not blame them, and take responsibility for his part in any low-level performance they display.

Within two weeks of implementing the new plan, Carlos went from receiving over 250 messages a day to less than 10.

Within four months, he went from working over 100 hours to less than 50 per week, and after six months, his firm made an extra $707,794 (approximately £596,734) profit compared to the same six months from the year before.

A major part of this was because Carlos learned to implement the context that there is never anything wrong, and that there is only ever something missing.

At this stage, I'd like to make clear that if a team member repeatedly operates at an unsatisfactory level of performance, shows no or little improvement, and you see there's nothing more you can take responsibility for in their lack of performance, it's possibly time to terminate their position or give them an alternative – such as a new position – that doesn't require them to demonstrate such a level of responsibility.

Own It

On to point 2. When you don't complete something well, or by when you said you would, don't hide it. Clear it up in a conversation.

It's very moving when someone openly owns their mistakes and says sorry to us.

We often feel no further need to defend ourselves against them or prove them wrong in an attempt to be right.

This is because owning mistakes takes a lot of courage. A person lets go of the need to be liked by us; they let go of needing to impress us; they face the consequences.

People who have the courage to own up to their mistakes display a truly attractive nature; they demonstrate the courage not to blame but to take responsibility. This is the foundational mindset for any truly great team member, manager, or leader.

Even though most people know this on some level, most business owners and employees (especially in the legal sector!) often avoid taking responsibility when they make a mistake, don't complete something well, or miss deadlines.

This is because most law firms are steeped in blame culture. It is much more common to hide and secretly blame circumstances when things don't go according to plan or mistakes are made than to openly take responsibility for them.

This is especially so in the legal sector because mistakes can often have profound consequences, and can gravely damage relationships with clients.

Not only this, but practising law is often about avoiding or solving big and painful problems for clients by using knowledge and the written word. Therefore, it is rare that problems are solved through verbal communication.

Because of this, naturally, most in the legal sector are not adept in verbal self-expression – especially when under pressure. Instead, they tend to lie low or aggressively shout at others out of survival.

This tendency to fight to survive underscores whatever it takes to impress others; it underscores the appearance that everything is being handled at all times.

The problem with behaving like this for long periods is that it becomes easy to lose touch with reality, to forget that behind the acting there is a human being. Someone with feelings, values, and often great ambition.

Over time, acting in such a way – always trying to impress and be right – becomes second nature, and we end up in a scenario where everyone is automatically acting the same with each other, behaving inauthentically and avoiding speaking openly.

This causes relationships with colleagues to become distant and causes us to experience a dissatisfying level of connection with those around us.

Then, when challenges arise (as they often do), it's natural that we continue doing what we have always done and automatically avoid taking responsibility. We hide our mistakes and hope that no one ever finds out.

When the owners of a law firm act like this, it encourages everyone else to behave the same. This is why the legal sector is renowned for having cultures that are not only full of blame but full of abuse and harassment from employers and employees to each other.

The way to ensure that you lead your firm out of a culture of blaming and into taking responsibility is by always looking at what *you* can take responsibility for first. Not only for *your* lack of performance or ineffective communication but also when it's clear that others have made a mistake.

From now on, carry out these steps as soon as you make a mistake, are late (or know you will be), or have broken a promise with someone:

1. Tell them the agreement you've broken.

2. Tell them how this negatively impacts them, your relationship, and the firm.

3. Tell them what you'll put in place that was missing to ensure you don't do this again. (Remember, there is never anything wrong and only ever something missing.)

4. Thank them for their patience and time.

5. For things like being late, text or call the person this affects.

If you start to do this communication openly, without blaming yourself or anyone else, over time you'll start to see other team members doing the same with you.

It's then much easier to speak openly, have everyone take responsibility for their actions, and work together to quickly solve problems. What naturally follows is a law firm that grows and becomes much more profitable.

Guilt

The above – owning your mistakes – applies to every mistake you'll make going forward; and if you are truly committed to creating a great law practice, there will be many mistakes!

There's no other way, but how do we handle mistakes and broken promises from our past?

The problem is that years of avoiding taking responsibility, alongside hiding and the blaming of others, causes us to carry the weight of judging ourselves; we subconsciously carry *guilt* into the interactions we have with others.

Often, this guilt is expressed through us feeling justifiably angry towards others, finding it difficult to express ourselves fully, and feeling that we are right in blaming others.

If you have something on your mind that you know you didn't handle well in the past, or you remember a mistake that badly impacted someone else's life and yet you got away with it, it's likely this is affecting your ability to lead others effectively much more than you are aware of.

This is because carrying such guilt causes us to be easily offended and quickly get angry towards others, so breaking free of such patterns is very effective at increasing our ability to effectively and compassionately lead others to operate at high levels of performance.

I've participated in advanced management and leadership programs where we had to write down everything we ever did that was dishonest or unkind towards another.

We then had to go find the people that those actions affected, speak to them, and do our best to clear up what we did by saying sorry.

I had a whole list to get through that went back to my teenage years, but after I courageously took responsibility for the past mistakes I'd made that I could think of, I set myself free from my past, and now I get to live with a deep sense of freedom every day.

What I'm saying is that this isn't easy (it took an extraordinary level of courage), but living a life where I have cleared up my past and regularly practise looking for what I can take responsibility for really has set me free.

So, from this moment onwards take responsibility for your past and present actions by *owning the conversation* whenever you are ineffective.

In doing so, you will not only transform the effectiveness of your leadership and the quality of your relationships, but also the lives of everyone else you work alongside and come into contact with.

Okay, It's Scary

The thought of taking responsibility and saying sorry for all your past mistakes and dishonest actions might seem overwhelming (and rightly so), but it doesn't need to happen all at once.

First, you need to genuinely want a wholly new and inspiring future, a future where you are seen by others as an extraordinary leader. Then, if this is what you choose, it's about creating a new way of moving at a pace that's right for you.

Equally, you need to get that if you keep treating your employees and team members as you've always done, nothing will change. Whatever challenges you currently face with your team's lack of performance, and your current level of success as a firm partner or owner, will continue to act as a ceiling that limits what you can achieve.

With regards to taking responsibility for bad performance from yourself and your team members as you become aware of it, I'm not suggesting you become someone who looks for problems and inefficient actions taken by others. What I am suggesting is that you become someone who never steps over an issue when you notice one.

Someone who runs at problems, someone who holds their team members to account and guides them to find solutions and end inefficiency, is going to be someone who achieves extraordinary results and impacts the lives of those around them in a fulfilling way.

Behind Their Back

On to point 3. Stop speaking badly about someone else behind their back. Campaign a policy across your firm for others to stop doing so, too.

When we say something about someone else that we wouldn't say to them directly, this is often gossip.

I say 'often' because, at times (e.g., when managers meet), we need to discuss the performance of a team member. Here, speaking behind someone's back is not gossip, it's a performance review!

In all cases, if you gossip about someone, it takes two. One to speak badly about someone (to judge them) and another to listen. Both are complicit in the act of gossiping. In doing so, both are encouraging others also to gossip.

This then becomes woven into the culture of your firm, and before long, everyone starts feeling like they need to be hyper-careful about anything they say in case it gets shared with someone else.

Such environments are the opposite of a 'thriving work culture' as they greatly damage performance. These environments are tense, restrictive, and don't feel safe to work in.

At your next meeting, when everyone in your firm is gathered, announce the following.

1. Explain that saying something about someone else in a way that is condescending or judgmental – and which we wouldn't say to them directly – is gossiping.

2. State that, from now on, any form of gossiping will not be tolerated in your firm.

3. Request that if anyone has a problem with any other colleague or employee, they first approach them directly to try to solve it.

4. Make it clear what the chain of command is, and – if needs be – offer a chain of command map that's available for everyone to see.

5. State that if the problem cannot be solved with the associated person directly, approach and speak to the person above them in their chain of command to get their support.

Once this is announced, the next thing is to continually support your firm's colleagues and employees to be open with each other, to not speak badly of each other behind each other's backs, and always to approach each other first to solve any problems that arise.

This will make your team better at communicating, especially when under pressure. More to the point, though, you will create an environment where people can speak openly with each other and trust that conversations won't go further without granted permission.

This creates a safe place to work, a place where people feel supported, and where they know that a support structure exists if problems cannot be solved. This will make them feel safe.

When you become skilled at listening and not expressing your frustration towards others, you will create an environment where your key team members will feel they can speak openly to you, too.

This freedom will give you a much better sense of what your employees and team members are dealing with. Accordingly, you can implement what is needed to prevent mistakes and inefficiencies from repeating, leading to an increase in your firm's profitability.

Team Responsibility Revision

- If you tend to express your anger towards colleagues and employees in your firm, stop doing this! Ensure you create an environment where your team members feel they can express things with you.

- Always be looking for what you can take responsibility for first, even when others are the ones who've made the mistake and not you.

- When you don't complete something well, or by when you said you would, don't hide it. Clear it up in conversation and make clear what you are putting in place so it doesn't happen again.

- Stop speaking badly about people behind their backs, and campaign a policy across your firm for others to behave likewise.

- Continually promote a context that *there is never anything wrong, there is only ever something missing*.

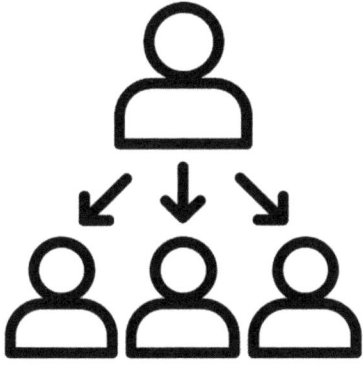

3. Requests & Accountability

If I'm wrong about this, contact me and tell me so! When you are contacted by one of your colleagues or clients wanting you to do something for them, do you immediately think, 'How am I going to fit this in?'

If so, it's ok. It's natural because you've always been committed to serving your clients well and ensuring they are pleased with your firm's work. Nonetheless, once a law firm partner or owner starts to delegate away their workload effectively, they move from thinking, 'How can I fit this in?' to 'Who can do this for me?'

'Who can do this for me?' needs to become the thought you brainwash yourself with as you go forward. It needs to be something you think about whenever you find yourself doing unsatisfying or tiring work – including admin, bookkeeping, or billable work.

If you don't start to think this way, you'll find yourself in the *Law Technicians Valley of Doom*. You'll continue to build a firm that relies on you to be profitable, and one day, you'll feel exhausted from doing the same thing every day.

Law firm partners and owners should *not* delegate business development before their billing work. In terms of greatly increasing their firm's profits, I've seen how my clients who *first* delegated away their admin and fee-earning work were the ones that really got ahead.

Business development needs to be the last thing you delegate away, as it's *you* that you want new clients to build a relationship with. In doing so, you maintain control over your firm's relationship with your clients.

Business development can be delegated away last: when you want to sell your firm, when you want to cash in and leave your firm, or when you want to become a member of an advisory board so you can participate less whilst enjoying the firm's success.

When you think about it, delegating your business development work so you can focus on doing more billable work is back-to-front. This is because your take-home profits will be greatly limited by your (in)capacity to complete billable work.

Not only this, but a focus on billable work means you cannot do business development yourself, elevate your team members' performance, or recruit ideal new members. Your firm won't grow (or will, but slowly at best), which puts you and your firm in danger of being taken down by your competitors.

To get the partners and equity partners of your firm on board in focusing on more business development versus billing, I suggest that you and all your firm partners reduce your required billing targets and introduce a commission (origination fee) on new business gained by each partner. Accordingly, when a partner secures a new client, they gain a 10 to 20% sales commission (origination fee).

This is a highly effective incentive!

Kate

When Kate, a solicitor and CEO of a firm specialising in compliance solutions for law firms, came to me, she led a small team. She was continually doing a lot of the fee-earning work to ensure the firm was profitable. As with most business owners, whenever new work would come in, she'd instantly think, 'How am I going to fit this in?'

As the reputation of her good work spread, she became so in demand for her services that she hit a point where she had to work well over 60 hours per week to keep up. Kate realised that she was soon going to need to work even longer – and put in more unsustainable hours – to keep up with the higher demand. That was when she contacted me to ensure that she could sustain high service levels without burning out.

Initially, the work we did was all about Kate getting used to not thinking, 'How am I going to fit this in?' but instead thinking, 'Who can do this for me?'

During the period that we worked together, Kate appointed key team members she could ask to take on some of the incoming existing and new client work. She recruited new senior members to take on the billable work she couldn't keep up with as demand for her service continued to grow.

This quickly transformed her experience from being a technician in her firm to a business owner. The new senior members freed up her time and Kate was then able to focus on recruiting more team members, doing more business development to further increase business, and setting the strategy to refine and standardise her firm's workflow procedures. As a result of all this, four months after we started working together, Kate posted this online:

"As I write this post on the final night of my first family sunshine holiday in more than 6 and 1/2 years. Not only is the business still running whilst I've been away and not working, but it's also driving forward. The team have secured new business, interviewed candidates to grow the team, appeared as industry guest speakers representing the company, created and published content and diverted disasters. All without my input whilst I've been away."

Not only this, but a further two months later, both Kate and her financial director reported to me that her firm had achieved over a 392% revenue increase in one year.

A major factor that made this possible for Kate was to first think, 'Who can do this for me?' and then she permitted herself to delegate her workload. Whenever she finds herself doing some admin or billable work, Kate now asks herself, 'Who can do this for me?'

Once Kate distinguished which of her members were best suited to delegate her billable work away to, she then made clear requests of each of them, and held them to account on what was agreed.

> " Of all the things I've done, the most vital is coordinating those who work with me and aiming their efforts at a certain goal. "
>
> **Walt Disney**

Leading versus Manipulating

When trying to get your team to do what you ask of them, what is the difference between 'leading' and 'manipulating' them?

The legal sector has a bad reputation for employees and associates being shouted at by owners and managers and often threatened with consequences such as being demoted or fired if they don't hit their targets.

The problem is that doing so greatly damages the relationship between the law firm owner or manager and the associate below them.

We all have experience of spending time with someone who easily loses their temper with us, who often criticises us, or who leaves us feeling like whatever we do is never good enough.

When we spend time with such people who leave us feeling this way, do we feel like telling them about our problems and challenges? Not at all. We become skilled at pretending that everything is ok; we do this out of a basic need to protect ourselves from being further disrespected and not treated kindly.

The same goes with everyone in your firm. If you treat them with disrespectful behaviour, such as shouting at them and using fear tactics (manipulating them) to get them to do what you want, it may work momentarily, but – soon enough – your team members will start to avoid you and avoid speaking openly to you.

The negative impacts of trying to lead team members who don't feel they can be open with you I covered in depth in the second chapter, entitled *Team Responsibility*, but I'd like to remind you that the impact of this is that your team members won't open up to you about the challenges they face. As a consequence, you'll never know what support or help they need to progress and succeed in their roles, which will cause them to experience a lack of progression and not feel valued. Ultimately, they will do the bare minimum work they can get away with, and – at some point – they will likely break their employment contract and leave your firm. As you know, this is frustrating and painfully expensive to deal with.

Manipulative behaviour uses fear to try to force others to do what you want...

- 'If you don't do this, your job is on the line.'

- 'If you don't do this, we're going to have serious words.'

- 'If I have to repeat myself once more, we are going to have major problems.'

If this is how you've been speaking to your team members, and you want to build a highly profitable firm while reducing your workload (and daily stress), I strongly suggest you *stop* speaking to team members in such ways. Stop using fear to try to force your team to do what you want.

As we can see, effective management is not manipulating others to take action, but using a balance of inspiration and accountability.

Although covered earlier in the book, let's take a moment to refresh the optimal strategy here. First, you need to get to know what each team member wants from your firm. You do this by using one-on-one meetings where you can ask:

- 'What made you take this job at this firm?'

- 'If anything could be made possible from you being at this firm, what would you love it to be?'

- 'Are you interested in more time off, more money, and/or becoming a partner here?'

No one is used to being asked such questions. We're all busy meeting demands, so team members may find answering these questions difficult. This is especially true if you have displayed anger towards the individual in the past and have spoken disrespectfully to them. If so, take responsibility for your past – say sorry and demonstrate being kind and compassionate towards them.

Though the past cannot be changed, you'll be surprised at how quickly you can heal many broken relationships with a little courage, and by taking full responsibility for your past actions and behaviours.

Even if you've treated your team members respectfully in the past, these questions can be difficult to answer, so it's wise to give each person plenty of time to answer the questions. Maybe ask for them to come back to you a week later, for example.

At a minimum, ask questions of each of your team members, or at least the heads of department, on a yearly basis. Request that each manager or head of department ask such questions of the team members they manage.

Then, throughout the year, maintain a context in your one-on-one conversations with each delegate, ensuring that each succeeds at what matters to them, alongside your firm's objectives, obviously. This is extremely valuable because the context behind *how* you speak to them will make them feel like they matter to you and that they are important to you. Consequently, this will make them more receptive to your requests and more willing to do what you ask.

> " Leadership is something you earn, something you're chosen for. You can't come in yelling, 'I'm your leader!' If it happens, it's because the other guys respect you. "
>
> **Ben Roethlisberger**
> **(Pittsburgh Steelers Quarterback)**

Clear Requests

Making clear requests is vital.

Without clear requests, team members can never be held to account and so can hide, freely perform at low levels, cost you a lot of money, and severely damage your firm's profitability.

Importantly, if requests aren't clear, it's not possible to know whether bad performance is due to a lack of your leadership or something that team members lack.

So, what is a clear request?

For a request to be clear, it must have all three of the following elements. Without them, it will be some strange form of communication that will usually lead to disappointing outcomes.

1. An unambiguous description of a measurable result you want someone to do.

Requesting that a team member "Go make that client happy" or "An email has come in from client 'X'… can you run with it?" are not clear requests. That is because there is no *precision* in what you are asking. If a team member takes action on these requests, chances are they'll deliver something that seems right in their minds, but not deliver the outcome you had in yours!

For a request to be clear, you need to ask for a measurable result to be delivered, such as:

- An email has come in from client 'X'. Can you phone them up, take detailed notes of what outcome they want from their situation, and email me a short, bulleted report?

- We have a commitment at this firm that all associates complete 100 hours of billable work per month. Can you do what it takes to get everyone in your team to hit this target?

- Can you compile a list of all the clients our firm has worked with since January 2021 into an Excel spreadsheet and then add a column after each – titled with all of the services we offer? Then, tick the services each client has received and email it to me so I can see which services we could offer them next.

All three of the above are the start of a clear request, but there are two more steps needed for each to be clear, which are as follows…

2. A clear time by which you want the task completed.

The problem with the above request examples is that they don't provide a time for each task to be completed by, or when they are to be implemented.

Let's say you have a client to whom you promised a piece of work by Friday 12pm, and you've asked an associate to do most of the work towards this. It's then Thursday evening (the night before), and you've still not had this associate submit their piece of the work.

You'll be thinking:

- 'Did they understand what I've asked of them?'

- 'Are they doing it?'

- 'Should I text or call them?'

The whole time you worry about whether this associate will get this piece of work to you on time, you cannot fully focus on other important work such as business development.

You'll be pacing around – worrying – and if you have additional work outstanding with other associates, you'll feel very stressed and anxious all the time, which is no way to live!

Instead, if you agree on a timeframe for work to be delivered, you can relax, focus on more important things, and check your inbox at the time of the deadline. If you still don't have that piece of work at the agreed time, pick up the phone and ask:

'Hi (associate name), we had an agreement you'd have this piece of work with me by 12pm today, and I've still not received it. When can you get it to me?'

You can then make a new agreement that works for you, and if needs be, call the client to ask if you can move the deadline to deliver the finished work to them.

3. Agreement from both parties on the result to be produced and the time frame.

Should you request a colleague to do something and the conversation gets interrupted shortly afterwards (or the meeting ends abruptly because of some pressing issue), leaving you with even the slightest sense they are not clear on what is requested of them or the time frame – there is a high chance they feel the same way!

Checking the colleague is clear on what you've asked of them may not be necessary for menial tasks, but for important tasks, it is wise to end requests by asking something like:

'Just to make sure we are both clear, can you confirm what I've requested of you?'

If the associate fails to add the timeframe, then ask!

'Ok, great. And by when?'

If any of the three elements in your requests are missing (i.e., 1. a measurable result you want delivering, 2. an exact time by when you'd like the result delivered, and 3. clarity between parties on what is being agreed), *a clear request has not been made*, which will usually lead to bad team performance and unfulfilled results.

All this may seem frustrating – and time-consuming to carry out – but if done correctly, the increase in productivity you'll see in each team member (while reducing your stress) and the associated increase in profitability will be worth your while.

So, what happens when you've done all this, and the associate you've instructed has not done what you've asked of them?

1. First, arrange a time to speak with the associate who has broken the agreement.

Many business owners and managers try to solve bad performance with an email dialogue. It is nowhere near as effective as verbal communication.

If you have regular one-on-one video calls or meetings scheduled with the associate (or head of department), bring the issue up at your next one.

2. When in a meeting or on a call with the associate, first acknowledge them for something they have done well or for their effort.

When we put ourselves under pressure to meet financial targets or goals, it can be easy to forget to speak to team members in a way that makes them feel appreciated.

With this in mind, it is vital to say something like:

'Jack, I just want to say that I enjoy working with you, and I see the effort you put in.'

Doing this gives you the opportunity to let any anger or frustration you feel with the individual dissipate whilst creating and maintaining a more enjoyable working relationship.

3. Next, remind the associate that, 'There is never anything wrong, there is only ever something missing.'

At this stage, the associate might be worried about what you'll say next. So, as I covered in chapter two, this is a prime moment to remind the delegate – *before you give them corrective instruction* – that there is never anything wrong and only ever something missing.

Doing this pre-empts the associate from feeling overly nervous and worrying about what you will speak about next.

4. Set an intention for the call or meeting.

You can say something like.

'In this meeting, I would like to look at how we can further increase what you can achieve in your role.'

This ensures that you are both clear on what objective you want to achieve as an outcome of the meeting.

5. Ask them if they agree that the specific agreement you had has been broken.

'Did you know we'd agreed that you would do X by Y time frame?'

When holding someone to account, it is always important to detail the broken agreement before going further. It is only when the delegate admits that the request you made of them was clear, and that they didn't fulfil what they agreed to do, that you can get to work on finding out *why* that delegate didn't do what was asked of them.

Whenever a team member lets you down, it's vital to first distinguish if it's your leadership that's missing, or something on their part that caused them not to deliver.

If the associate says they were not clear on what was asked of them, you can generously take responsibility for your lack of clear communication.

'Thanks so much for enabling me to see that I have not been clear in what I asked of you. From now on, I will ensure that my requests to you are clear. Each time, I will check that you are clear on what I've asked of you.'

Whenever you discover that it's *your* leadership that is missing – such as a lack of communication on your behalf – and you actively commit to putting in place what was missing on *your* side, the greater your skill will become in guiding your team members to do the same when they don't fulfil their agreements.

6. If they agree that they broke the specific agreement, acknowledge them for their courage in owning this. Then, ask them leading questions to find a solution so they don't make the same mistake again.

As compassionate as you try to be when holding associates to account for their broken agreements, the conversation can easily become awkward, so it's sensible to keep guiding the delegate away from blaming themselves, other colleagues, or circumstances. Instead, work with them to purely investigate and put in place what was missing to ensure the same doesn't happen again.

Speaking with the associate and simply telling them what to do (so they don't make the same mistake again) isn't very effective. They will likely agree to whatever you suggest in an attempt to please you in the moment while avoiding a full commitment to what you suggest.

Instead, it's much more effective to ask them leading questions to identify solutions, such as:

'What got in the way of you not completing this on time?'

'What can you see is missing that – if you put it in place – would ensure this doesn't happen again?'

After you ask such questions, hold the silence! Relax into the awkward silence between you and let them struggle to find the answer. Only prompt them with a suggestion if they really can't think of what solutions to suggest.

The more you do this, the better they will become at solving problems themselves, which means less hand-holding from you.

When the team member distinguishes what was missing, or you *both* arrive at what caused them not to complete the task, and when they (not you) come up with a solution to ensure the same thing doesn't happen again, they are much more likely to implement it. They (instead of you) have thought of the solution, and they are far less likely to repeat the same mistake… saving you the frustration of having to handle the same mistake again.

To be clear, you 'telling them' what to do going forward is nowhere near as effective as them discovering and suggesting the solution.

Suppose the associate lets you down by making the same mistake more than twice, or doesn't do the same task you've requested of them for more than two weeks in a row. In that case, you need to implement bolder management (accountability) communication to ensure they have a breakthrough in ending their repetition of the same mistakes.

As human beings, we only ever change our ways when the discomfort of what we're experiencing is greater than the discomfort we feel towards doing something about it.

For instance, look at our health. If we have a habit of eating bad food and drinking a lot, there's no real need to change what we do until – one day – we look in the mirror and are shocked at how we look, or we receive a health scare from a doctor.

Often, it's only then that we feel motivated to do something about our habit of eating bad food and drinking a lot.

The same goes for any employee or associate. If they feel they can keep repeating mistakes and continually not do what they agree to – while not having any sort of consequence to deal with – they'll often not change anything and will keep repeating the same mistakes.

For this reason, when your team members repeatedly let you down, you need to step up your management practice. You do this by practising what I call 'impact work'. This is done by asking questions such as:

'How do you think your non-completion on time impacts our firm?'

'How does you not doing what we agree impact our relationship?'

'And what is the impact of this on your future in this firm?'

Some of these may seem like a threat but they are genuine questions that are aimed to lead the delegate into *becoming aware* of the unwanted side effects of their lack of effective operation in your firm.

When asking the associate these questions, courageously hold the silence after you've asked them. Let them face the awkwardness they feel, and don't let your own emotions get in the way of doing this.

If you interrupt their thinking and their answers to these questions, you will be stealing the opportunity for them to experience a breakthrough in their performance. As a consequence, they will likely gain fewer opportunities in your firm and in their career as a whole.

> " If you want to lift yourself up, lift up someone else – and trust they will do the same. "
>
> **Booker T. Washington**

When you ask such questions to someone who refuses to cooperate, you will allow them to become aware of the impact their ineffective actions are having on your relationship, plus your firm's and their success. The realisation of the impact of their actions will often be what is needed to shock them into increasing their reliability as a team member or employee.

Doing this might seem like manipulation, but it isn't. It's simply guiding your team members to become aware of what they were previously unaware of.

If what they discover leaves them feeling shocked, that's something for them to deal with, and you can always be there to support them should they need help.

When the associate understands the depth of how badly impactful their actions (or lack of them) have been on your firm, your relationship, and their future, you can be confident they won't repeat the mistake again.

Throughout this process, don't forget to remind the associate that there is never anything wrong and there is always only something missing.

This is so the conversation continues to be aimed at discovering and implementing what was missing in order to avoid the same mistakes being made.

7. Ask them to see what was missing so they can take action to avoid this from happening again.

This has already been covered, but only move past this point when the team member has suggested something new to implement going forward; something that you both can see will most likely ensure the mistake doesn't happen again.

Only when you *both* see this can you declare the problem as solved and end the meeting or speak about the next subject.

On some occasions, it's difficult to see what would prevent the same mistake from happening again. When this happens, note down that it still needs resolving and bring it up again in the next one-on-one meeting with the associate.

8. Acknowledge them for making an effort to work on their performance.

Such conversations are often hard work for both you and the team members, so it's wise to reward them again with further acknowledgement for being involved in such a challenging conversation. You can say something like:

'Thanks for taking the time to solve this. You've been great in working this through with me.'

Remember that manipulating your team with pressure and fear tactics never works well in the long run. Instead, implement what I've covered here to effectively manage them by ensuring that your team members consistently feel valued and respected by you.

To ensure this, and that you are not manipulating your associates, always give them the freedom to choose what to do (or say) after you've requested something from them.

The options you must always provide are:

• Accept

- Decline
- Counteroffer

You might make particular mention of these options when you make a request and the associate starts to give lots of excuses as to why they can't do what you ask of them.

Or maybe when they start to talk about superficial details which are not moving the conversation forward, you can say something like:

'You are making some fair points here. Regarding this request, do you accept, decline, or counteroffer?'

This way, the conversation will always move forward effectively.

If, when making a request, the associate simply says, 'Got it. I'll have that done for you by 6 pm tomorrow', then that's settled.

If they reply and decline what you've asked of them, you can have a conversation to understand why there is resistance and lead them to suggest a solution that would satisfy both of you.

Alternatively, you might both see that your request is better undertaken by other team members.

Sometimes, team members might agree to what you ask of them but will say they can't do so by the deadline you set. Here, they can make a counteroffer, and you can negotiate an alternative deadline that works for both of you.

Whatever the case, the choice to accept, decline, or counteroffer in return for what you ask of them will keep them moving forward effectively.

On some occasions, you might find that associates refuse to agree to deadlines or decline many of the requests you make of them. If so, carry out some impact work with them and ask them things like:

'If you can't agree on a timeframe for completing the work that's asked of you, how does this impact the firm's ability to meet our client's deadlines?'

'If you continue to refuse to do the work that's asked of you – that we know you are fully capable of doing – how will that impact the kind of opportunities that are offered to you?'

At some stage, through questions such as these, they should become aware of how ineffective it is for them not to cooperate with you. This should prompt useful suggestions so that you can negotiate with them and arrive at a way of working together that suits you both.

Requests and Accountability Revision

- A clear request has a clear description of the task, a time frame, and agreement from everyone involved.

- Manipulation through fear tactics is not effective. Rather, inspiring people to take action gains much better results.

- To make sure no one is being manipulated across your firm, always ensure there is a context in which anyone in your firm can accept, decline, or counteroffer any request that is made of them.

- When holding someone to account for something they didn't do as promised, don't tell them what to do (i.e., advise them) but guide them (i.e., lead them) to tell you what happened and suggest a solution to stop the same from happening again. Doing this is much more likely to ensure they implement the solution they think of.

- Create structures that hold your team members to account for their agreements while also continually supporting them to ensure they succeed at both what matters to them and in meeting the targets that make them most valuable to fulfilling your firm's objectives.

Lana Sheppard Case Study

In this case study, we discover how effective delegation can benefit a different type of business. The lessons and insights that Lana shares below apply equally to law firms.

Lana Sheppard was once the owner of a bookkeeping and payroll firm. At the time, she was exhausted and worked very long hours. Nine months later, after implementing many of the leadership and management strategies covered in this book at her firm, not only did she delegate all of her billable work and most of her business operations to both existing and new team members, but she also sold her business for the sum of money she always wanted. She then travelled and spent time across the world.

Lana now shares the learning through her GiveUp Series books and has recently started a non-profit organization in Canada to raise funds for a business technology classroom in the Philippines to teach bookkeeping to Filipino business college students.

Lana's background is all about numbers and accounting – the same as most law firm owners. She once charged herself and her team out at a billable hourly rate.

"I was overwhelmed and extremely stressed," she explains. "I managed a business with 18 staff members and around 600 active clients, handling bookkeeping and payroll. Constantly chasing tax deadlines, year-end deadlines, and client demands, I had to manage payroll for over 200 companies weekly. Day after day, I never knew if the light at the end of the tunnel was hope or another challenge. It was both overwhelming and exhausting; I had been doing this for over 15 years while also raising my kids alone as a single parent.

"I'd got to the point where I didn't want to feel anymore. I just needed to get stuff done. I got to the point where I just had blinders on, and I knew what my task list was every day. I'd often crawl into my bed in the early morning after working late into the night, then wake up after having hardly slept and I was off doing tasks. I didn't spend a moment of the day on me or take a breath.

"I was working weekends as well as doing all-nighters. There were times I'd leave the office at six in the morning, shower, and go back to work by eight o'clock when staff came in. I'd worked all night, and then I'd be busy with staff all day.

"By five o'clock, when everybody else went home, my day would start, and I'd do all my administrative work. I was getting 150 to 200 emails a day. It was exhausting, absolutely exhausting."

So, did Lana know she was in trouble?

"Yes and no. I think you have this kind of state of denial. You really don't want to admit it. You kind of lie to yourself and think, 'Ah, no. It'll be fine. Next week will be better.' So, I knew, but I didn't want to go there because I knew it would take work to get myself out of that condition and move into a new one."

Did Lana try to look for solutions or ways out of her situation?

"Oh yeah. I'd taken courses. I took courses which gave me light bulb moments, and I thought, 'This sucks. I don't want to stay here anymore.' From there, I got myself mentally prepared to dig in and start doing the work in a committed way.

"Once I got clear on what I truly wanted – which was to sell my business – it gave me that extra drive to push through the rest of the challenges and make it happen. That's really the biggest thing.

"Dan helped me push through some limiting beliefs and break free of my own hesitations caused by a lack of confidence and self-esteem."

Lana had dreamed of selling her business for seven years, but her self-limiting ways of thinking had constrained her; she never had the courage to find out how to sell her business and follow through. Instead, Lana had built a firm that constantly relied on her to keep operating because she'd developed a deep habit of trying to do all her client work herself and not delegating it to her team. During conversations, Lana revealed that she had read over 300 books in two-and-a-bit years in order to learn how to take the business forward so it could be sold. Her take on this is valuable:

"Is knowledge power? No, knowledge isn't power. It's knowledge put into action that's power!"

Some of the initial work Dan did with Lana was laying out all the roles for everybody in her business, determining what was best done by who, and then looking at everything that Lana had to do on a daily basis to lead everyone to operate effectively in their roles. This included making clear requests and holding team members to account for fulfilling what was agreed.

It was the fundamental skill of delegating the majority of her workload to her team members and preparing them that made all the difference because – *at this point* – Lana was able to really focus on making her business as profitable as possible. And she did, into seven figures.

"The sales revenue of the business hit seven figures, which for women entrepreneurs is a huge achievement. Only 2% of women entrepreneurs around the world have seven-figure businesses, which I was super stoked about.

"I had the business just doing bookkeeping, and it was then one of the largest in Canada. Yet I didn't have accountants working for me, and we just strictly did bookkeeping and payroll, which was unheard of. Most bookkeeping firms have one or two people, and they may hit $300,000 to $400,000 in sales per year at the most. So, what I had built over 14 years was unique in itself, but the best part was that – through effective delegation – I'd not only increased its revenue and profit but had a team reliably taking the weight off my shoulders, and I started to get my life back."

Lana was finally in a great position because she'd built a business that was highly attractive to buyers. Not only was it running reliably and profitably, but it didn't require its owner, Lana, to keep operating it.

After the sale was complete, Lana then coached and mentored the new owner to take over from her.

"I spent X number of hours a week mentoring her. It was a nightmare because of COVID, and everything was upside down with all the government subsidies, but after the first year of owning this business, she came out the other end and in a good position, as the firm had hardly lost a client."

By this stage, Lana had successfully sold her once-incredibly exhausting business for the sum of money she always wanted; her old business was full of clients, so the new buyer was happy, and she'd removed herself fully while gaining decent profits from the sale.

"I now have, like, zero stress. I can get up in the morning, and I don't have to have my feet hit the ground and run, or think about whose books I need to work on. I can get up in the morning and enjoy my mornings. I sleep well at night. I don't have the business on my mind 24/7; I no longer have to work on it all the time and now have lots of free time to myself."

"I'm now having the time of my life because I get to give it back to people in a way that really fulfils me. And I think that's important for us who are older, doing the succession exit plan – that sort of thing – to share it down.

"Figuring out that vision is so important. What held me back was my limiting beliefs and not knowing what I was going to do once I sold my business. When Dan helped me figure that out, that gave me the fuel to go because I felt inspired by what I discovered I wanted. Business is hard, but it's fulfilling and satisfying.

"It's important to have that vision nailed down. You need to know it, and it's not just your business vision; it's your whole life vision. You need to know in all aspects of your life – what do you want? And where do you want to be? And figure that out because, really, a business is only one of those vehicles to get you living the life you want, and that's the difference between working in your business and on your business. The revenue you're going to have from that business will be the vehicle to give you the life you want."

It was confirmed with Lana that she managed to delegate 90% of her roles and then sell her bookkeeping business for over £440,000, which is something she had tried to achieve for seven years before working with Dan.

4. Delegation Structures

A law firm owner who succeeds in building a highly profitable business – while having the free time to focus on what matters to them – implements *proactive* management, not reactive management.

So, what is the difference between proactive and reactive management?

I'll give you a set of examples of what it looks like when a law firm owner is *reactively* trying to manage everything in their firm:

1. They make themself available and contactable at all times.

2. They don't set and communicate boundaries.

3. They usually give answers to issues.

4. They advise instead of leading team members to find and offer solutions to the challenges they face.

5. They don't schedule regular one-on-one calls with key team members or heads of departments.

6. They don't make clear requests by including a measurable result and a time frame that's agreed upon.

7. They don't have regular set times to train their team members to become aware of their mistakes so they can stop repeating them.

Law firm owners who look like the list above leave themselves constantly 'reacting' to situations as they arise. They often have to stop what they are doing to handle something. This causes them to break their concentration repeatedly across the day, so they often need to stop and restart what they are trying to do.

At the end of a day's work like this – trying to do billing work and continually being interrupted with urgent matters from associates – most law firm owners end up absolutely exhausted and with a feeling that they haven't done anything productive with their time.

> **"** To win in the marketplace you must first win in the workplace. **"**
>
> **Doug Conant**
> **(Former President and CEO of**
> **Campbell Soup Company)**

Habib

An existing client referred Habib to me. A brilliant lawyer and the owner of a 75-person firm, he was in a great position as he was the sole owner of his company, which had five departments, each offering a different legal service. Each department also had a manager in place who was responsible for hitting their own billing targets.

The problem was that even though Habib had these five managers in place, he was exhausted from having to supervise everything to ensure the firm ran well. Because he was constantly having to handle urgent problems, Habib didn't have time to see how he could increase his firm's profits.

When we started working together, he told me how he was receiving over 50 emails a day from his team members, which he said he didn't need to receive, read, or have anything to do with. Yet, he allowed this to continue!

One of the first things we did was to get Habib to start expressing himself fully, setting boundaries with each head of a department. This was because it was these heads of departments who were supposed to be responsible for ensuring Habib was no longer copied into each email that he didn't need to be.

Until this point, he was replying by email to each person who copied him into these emails, requesting they didn't do so again and that they use their head of department for queries. I guided Habib to see that emails are easily ignored and as such, the individuals copying him into these emails were not being held to account effectively. They each lacked a regular verbal conversation, and so the problem continued.

What was missing was that Habib didn't have regular weekly one-on-one calls with each head of department, so that was the first thing we put in place.

On these calls, I suggested Habib make each head of department ensure that no one in their team ever copied Habib into an email again, and that if they felt they needed to, to ask their head of department to step in to help instead.

Then, week by week, we saw he was being copied into fewer and fewer emails that didn't require him. As time went on, if Habib was copied into an email he didn't need to be, he made a note and brought it up on the next weekly call with the relevant head of department. In the call, he asked the head of department to ensure their team member didn't do so again.

As a result, Habib now receives under half the number of emails he did previously, saving him over 30 minutes per day (the time he was previously spending having to read and delete all the emails that didn't concern him).

Here are the delegation structures you need to have in place to move out of reactive management and into much more profitable, proactive management:

Set regular one-on-one calls with key team members.

As with Habib, scheduling regular one-on-one calls is one of the first things I work on with my clients.

When they are not in place, it's very difficult to give associates and managers the time they need to become truly valuable team members. This is because it's impossible to consistently distinguish what each team member's challenges are, or to help them find and implement the solutions to overcome those challenges.

I've come to see that there really is *no other way* than leading regular one-on-one calls to lead and manage team members effectively.

Before working with me, some of my clients said they had regular weekly group meetings, but such meetings never offered the support the associates needed to become superstar fee-earners, which is why they contacted me.

The benefits of leading regular one-on-one video calls or in-person meetings are extraordinary when it comes to increasing the reliability of team members hitting their billing targets and taking the weight off your shoulders.

You might be thinking that you speak to some of your managers and heads of department many times a day already, so don't see the value in this. Such regular conversations about meeting client needs, or to work on some aspect of a project, are not the same. In these conversations, there is rarely any extra time to re-evaluate the broader picture, which is why this needs to be regularly scheduled.

How often should these one-on-one meetings or video calls happen?

Above, I talk about weekly meetings because I've found that a weekly timeframe is optimal. What may vary, of course, is the length of those meetings. If you are having regular meetings with a head of department who is already consistently hitting their billing targets, and is effectively managing everyone below them to hit theirs, then you may only need a 15 or 20-minute call each week to check in with them.

However, if the head of department you are managing isn't hitting their agreed billing targets, and neither are the associates in their team, then a one-hour meeting per week is needed.

This may seem like a lot, but don't forget you want them to *think* and *behave* like you if they are to run your law firm profitably for you. Spending time with them in this way is *the only way* it will happen and – I guarantee you – the rewards of giving your team members such support are astounding.

This is because you'll see that in only in a matter of weeks of implementing this with each of your key employees or your heads of department, the mount of interruptions you receive will radically reduce which, even with all your weekly one-on-one meetings scheduled you'll see you gain a lot of your time back to focus on more important activities.

For this to be effective, don't forget to request that, unless necessary, they should not contact you or ask you for anything outside of these meetings.

Naturally, team members will have things they will need to contact you about when they are stuck... but for all other problems they face, they need to do their best. They can ask others to help solve issues, or they can write each problem down and bring it to you in their next one-on-one session.

Carlos

The above – 'don't contact me unless entirely necessary' – is one of the requests my client Carlos made of the key team members he'd arranged one-on-one calls with. He was astounded at how quickly this freed up his time; he no longer had to handle a large number of emails and calls that were not urgent or important, which wasted his time. This is one of the great benefits of this structure.

This is what to cover in your weekly one-on-one meeting with each key team member:

1. Acknowledge them for the work they do well, or at least the effort you see them put in.

Doing this gives team members the opportunity to feel valued by you before giving them corrective instruction or making more requests of them. Also, acknowledge each team member at the end of any one-on-one meeting for their time and effort.

All this ensures that team members feel continually rewarded for what they do, which – in turn – will make them so much easier to work with and less likely to look for a new position elsewhere.

2. See whether the agreements made in the previous week's meeting have been fulfilled or broken.

Whilst reading this book, and if you've fully understood how vital it is to make clear requests with agreed deadlines, you might have questioned how it's possible to track all your agreements with team members, and how they do what you ask of them by the agreed time.

If so, I find that keeping an online document, such as a Google Doc, and then dating a new column each week works well.

This document can then be shared on a screen each week during one-on-one meetings (which I cover how to do effectively later), and you can take notes on what agreements and deadlines have been set each week.

Then, each week, you can check to see what agreements have been met or broken. Remember, if an agreement has been broken, you need to first check that they were clear on what was agreed. When they agree they haven't done what they promised, you can rule out something missing in your communication.

As you do this, keep the conversation light and assure them that there is never anything wrong and only ever something missing!

The art here is to guide associates by asking them leading questions (not by telling them what to do) that generate suggestions as to what they can put in place to ensure promises don't get broken again.

Associates will remember what *they* come up with, and this helps ensure the same broken promises don't happen again.

3. Review work together, and train team members so they do not repeat mistakes.

This can seem very laborious at first, but clients who have implemented this (typically seeing the benefits in just six to eight weeks) have noticed a radical increase in an associate's ability to deliver much-improved work consistently.

To do this effectively, ask that the associate, manager, or head of department that you want to train sends you their completed piece of work several days before it needs to be submitted to your client.

When it arrives with you to be checked, highlight any sections that have mistakes, then save that as a separate copy. You can then amend the mistakes on the original and submit the work to your client if needs be.

Then, when on the next one-on-one call, you can show the piece of work that you've marked up and ask them (not tell them) why you've marked each piece.

When they get stuck and can't see why, prompt them with a suggestion or – if you're really going nowhere – give them the answer.

As I've said before, it's holding that awkward silence while someone thinks that causes them to become skilled at thinking for themselves and coming up with solutions.

In doing this, and as I've also mentioned before, it becomes much more likely they'll avoid repeating the same mistake, and the outcome will be much more effective than if you simply told them the correct thing to do.

If you maintain this process with an associate or head of department over a four- to eight-week period, I guarantee you'll be astounded at how much less work you need to mark as containing mistakes. Soon enough, you'll have such confidence in them carrying out good work that you can step down to only randomly check their work.

If you implement co-reviewing client work with another team member (which I highly suggest you do, especially when you have someone earmarked to take over the laborious work you no longer want), set a different time for each fee earner to submit their work to you, so you don't get too much work to review at once.

Also, ensure you leave enough time for you or your fee earner to amend client work before release.

The advanced stage of this process is then requesting the people that you've trained in this way – who have become reliable at delivering a high standard of work – to take over the checking of other associates, managers, or heads of departments, instead of you. Getting this right can truly elevate your whole team's ability to deliver great work to your clients while saving you time.

4. Make new, clear requests of team members to take over your fee-earning work.

Once you've gone through the promises they've broken, and worked with them to prevent any reoccurrences, and if they seem ready to step up, you can think about asking associates to take fee-earning work off your plate.

Use the ongoing one-on-one calls to check they have everything they need, and offer training (as appropriate) so they become proficient in doing the work you ask of them.

With this in place, your operational hours will reduce while the profitability of your firm will increase.

This is extremely rewarding because you have freed up time to offer more associates your support – further increasing their value to your firm – or you can now go out and win new and inspiring business opportunities.

5. Request ideal workflows to be written down for everyone to follow.

In the great book 'The E-Myth Revisited' by Michael E. Gerber, which is all about business systemisation, he writes, *"Documentation says, 'This is how we do it here.'*

"Without documentation, all routinized work turns into exceptions.

"Documentation provides your people with the structure they need and with a written account of how to get the job done" in the most efficient and effective way. It communicates to the new employees, as well as to the old, that there is a logic to the world in which they have chosen to work, that there is a technology by which results are produced. Documentation is an affirmation of order."

In other words, if you don't have documented procedures in place in your firm for how you do things, everyone will carry out their own processes and procedures in a slightly different way each time.

This means that you can never find the inefficiencies in their workflow; you can never see what is wasting their time; you can never see what they need to cut out or do more of.

Also, if an associate ever leaves and they haven't adhered to a manual/handbook on how they do what they do, the onboarding process of their replacement will quite simply be painful.

The newcomer will need to work everything out on their own and even come up with new processes and procedures from scratch, just to bridge the gap in the workflow from the associate who's left.

With this in mind, when an associate has worked out general workflows that enable them to reliably deliver a good standard of work, get them to write down – step by step – what they do.

Then, in the future, should they start to make mistakes or the standard of their work drops, you can refer back to the workflow processes and procedures they wrote out and check that they've stuck to what worked in the past.

At this stage, you might discover that it's other processes or procedures that have been changed by other members of your firm which are affecting this associate's workflow.

As such, and utilising the context that *there is never anything wrong and only ever something missing*, you can both become detectives to discover and put in place what is missing to solve the breakdown. Then, request that the associate updates their written procedures with what they are going to implement going forward, and go again. As you have regular one-on-one calls scheduled with them each week, you can then check they are back on track and offer more support as and when needed.

6. Communicate your boundaries.

It's important to let your team members know what your boundaries are, and it will sometimes take some self-enquiry for you to determine what they are before you can communicate them.

One boundary could be that as soon as they know they can't meet a deadline, they need to text you so that you can make new arrangements.

Another boundary might be scheduling particular times when you are not to be disturbed. Put them on a shared calendar and ensure that everyone knows to leave you be during these periods. Now, you have carved out sacred, quiet periods when you can get your most important work done.

Another boundary might be requesting that half-finished work does not get submitted to you; you expect work to be completed before it is shared. Instead, associates are to tell you when they can't finish the piece on time. On the next one-on-one meeting, you can then investigate what has happened with them, and support them to ensure the same thing doesn't happen again.

Group Calls and Meetings

Now that you've got a good sense of how to use your time in one-on-one meetings, we'll look at group video calls/group meetings.

These are vital to give people a feeling of being part of something great – being a valued team member and intrinsically part of something that requires active team membership.

Group meetings are also a great opportunity to acknowledge and celebrate a team member's participation and give reminders of firm-wide targets.

These firm-wide meetings are good to have once a week as this keeps momentum going, but soon enough, you may not need to attend every single one. You may find that having a weekly team call with only your heads of departments or managers can be a great way to share ideas and create further effective teamwork and collaboration.

This is what to cover in your weekly group video calls or in-person meetings:

1. Always start by having fun!

Doing this helps break down the barriers between team members and thus helps maintain good working relationships between them.

You can start the meetings by asking:

'Who did something silly last weekend?'

'Anyone get up to something new?'

or

Mention something funny you've seen in the news and ask if anyone else has seen it and what they think.

The idea is just to get team members interacting in a fun and relaxed way.

2. Acknowledge team members for their work.

More on this in the next section.

3. Take responsibility for your and the team's low performance, and lead them to create new commitments to solve this.

If you want to effectively move your firm's culture from one where everyone blames 'something else' for their lack of performance (which is exhausting to manage) and instead create a culture of taking responsibility – a culture where team members own their mistakes, find solutions, and implement them – you need to lead by example first.

Though it takes a lot of courage, your weekly firm-wide Zoom or in-person meeting is a perfect time to demonstrate this, and will be very effective in developing deep respect for you from team members.

You can say something like.

'I realised today that I am often late for meetings. This isn't effective because we have a commitment in this firm to be true to our word, and to do what we say, and I haven't been doing this. It's then not fair if I hold you to account for your agreements. So, from now on, I'm going to ensure I don't have meetings back to back so I can log into each Zoom meeting five minutes early, and ensure I am on time for everyone. Is that clear for everyone?'

Can you sense how effective this will be? You are leading your team members by example. By walking the walk, team members will know how important it is to be on time.

In a future group meeting, you might at some point also say something like:

'Before we go any further, I see that many of you are struggling to hit your billing targets. I take responsibility for this as I realise that I haven't been working closely enough with your department heads to give you the support you need. This must be very frustrating to those of you who have been struggling with this.

'Going forward, this will be something I'll be covering in each of my one-on-one weekly meetings with each of your department heads (or managers); together, we'll distinguish what is missing and give you the support you need.'

" Leadership consists of nothing but taking responsibility for everything that goes wrong and giving your subordinates credit for everything that goes well. **"**

Dwight D. Eisenhower

---

4. Lead the team to implement solutions to close the gaps in their performance.

Often, holding individual team members to account is better done in the privacy of one-on-one meetings. Sometimes, however, you might notice some firm-wide ineffectiveness, such as everyone not saving files to the firm's workflow management system. This is a breakdown I recently worked with a client to solve.

You might say something like.

'I notice that a lot of current cases have key documents missing. I see the documents are being emailed to the client but not being stored on our system. This means that if we ever hit complexities on a case or there is an inspection of our procedures, we could be in major trouble. Who can suggest a solution to this?'

You would then lead a conversation between everyone to arrive at a collective agreement that all files must be saved in the relevant project on your firm's workflow management system.

When everyone is involved in arriving at such a solution – by having to at least think about what the solution could be – they are much more likely to implement the agreed solution.

In your next one-on-one meeting with each manager or head of department, you can request they each remind each associate below them of this new requirement.

This 'open house' procedure is effective in solving all firm-wide problems and inefficiencies you notice.

> **"** I've always found that the speed of
> the boss is the speed of the team. **"**
>
> **Lee Iacocca**

5. Announce updates that will affect all or most team members.

These announcements might be adjustments in the billing targets everyone is to achieve. Announcing them helps each manager to effectively hold their team members to account in their future one-on-one meetings with each of them.

Other useful announcements are changes in processes and management, and reassuring everyone that everything will continue as usual. Doing this gives your employees a sense of feeling valued and that they are important to you and your firm.

Announcing new firm-wide bonus schemes or rewards for everyone hitting their billing targets can also create a sense of enthusiasm and inclusivity for those involved.

6. Lead collective conversations about your company's values and mission statement.

Having company values and a mission statement in place for everyone to follow may not seem important, *but it is*.

It's too much for me to cover how to create them in this book (doing so is a whole other topic), but if you don't have them in place, I suggest digging into how to create and implement them. When everyone in a law firm adheres to values such as 'being client-centric, inclusive and compassionate', it can create a truly thriving work environment.

Also, have a mission statement to work towards (i.e., a target), such as:

'We are the number one conveyancing firm in our county. We are renowned for our reliability and impact on local communities.'

or:

'We are an award-winning commercial law firm that is renowned for solving complex challenges faced by the UK's greatest businesses.'

These intentions will help you to lead everyone to work towards the same objective; effectively, they will pull everyone into collaborating as a team.

When team members are informed of such company values or mission statements, they can often feel like they are being told something that doesn't *mean anything to them*. The impact is that they won't feel that their firm's values or mission statement particularly applies to them, and instead applies more (or only) to the firm owners.

For this reason, it's unlikely they'll feel inspired by the firm's values or mission statement, and won't feel disposed to bringing it to life in their actions.

The way to solve this is to make your firm members feel like they are part of the process that underpins the creation of values or mission statements.

I suggest reviewing and offering everyone a part in re-writing them once a year through longer firm-wide meetings. It's a good idea, however, to have new employees and team members feel part of them right away.

The way you do this is by – once a month, on one of your weekly firm-wide Zoom calls or in-person meetings – requesting someone in your firm to read out your firm's values and mission statement, and then asking your team members what they mean to them or what they have noticed about them in a new way that they hadn't noticed before.

After they are read out, you could ask:

'Which of these values are important to you and why?'

'What does practising these values make possible for us and our clients?'

'When you hear the mission statement, what did you notice in it that you didn't notice before?'

The objective in asking these questions is to initiate a firm-wide conversation where people share their thoughts and ideas.

Everyone, including those who don't seem to participate, will find themselves thinking of what they might say or add which, in turn, will raise their awareness of your firm's values and mission statement.

Why is it so important to have a chain of command agreed and in place? What is the best way to set this up?

It can be very frustrating for an associate if they have two or more managers they report to, and they experience conflicts between what one manager asks of them versus the other.

The *only time* an associate can effectively be managed by more than one manager is if they specifically report to each individual on a different kind of work or project.

Even so, it's not effective for an associate or team member to be mentored and held to account for their overall performance by more than one manager at a time. Put another way, it works best when each team member or associate only has regular one-on-one support calls scheduled with one manager at a time.

When a firm's structure is set correctly, you'll have a neat pyramid structure with the law firm owners, partners, CEOs, or MDs at the top.

Then, everyone in your firm has one person above them who predominantly manages and supports them with weekly one-on-one meetings.

For a small law firm, this ideal chain of command could look something like this:

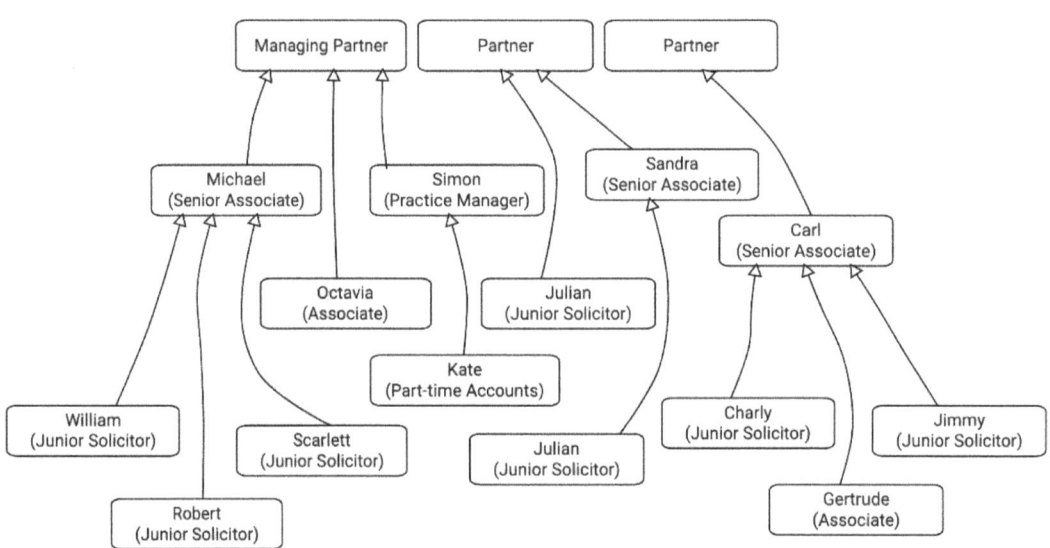

As you can see, with the firm owners at the top, everyone in the firm below them has one other person they mainly report to, and have a weekly one-on-one call or meeting with.

Also, as you see, not all firm members report to all partners. Instead, the partners each have a senior member below them who then manages the junior associates below them. This is important to set, otherwise – as a partner – you can end up with too many one-on-one calls per week, which will take your attention away from important activities such as business development, recruiting, and the provision of extra training as and when needed.

In this example, the managing partner leads three one-on-one calls per week, the partner next to him leads two per week, and the partner on the right leads a single one-on-one call or meeting per week.

In regards to this example, it may still be that some of the associates report to more than one senior member (and also maybe to one of the partners for extra training and support when needed or about a specific project they are both working on). But the crux of this structure is that each team member has *one* member with whom they have a weekly one-on-one call or meeting to hold them accountable.

This configuration – where everyone has a weekly one-on-one call with someone more senior in the firm – can continue to work as the firm grows. It means that everyone, *and I mean everyone in the firm,* will always have someone who ensures they are both succeeding in meeting their agreements and getting what they want out of their position in the firm.

This organisational structure is also very effective in ensuring that no one in your firm is hiding or pretending to be busy.

Another benefit is that when new firm-wide targets are set, or operational changes or system improvements made, they are acted on from top to bottom effectively.

This will make your firm agile and able to solve unforeseen challenges as they arise quickly.

Delegation Structures Revision

1. Move from reactive to proactive leadership.
2. Set regular weekly one-on-one calls or meetings, and request that each head of department, manager, or senior associate does so with each of the people they manage below them.

3. Request that – unless necessary – you are only to be contacted during one-on-one meetings.

4. Set regular, weekly, firm-wide video calls or meetings.

5. Co-review work with associates and train team members to ensure they avoid repeating the same mistakes.

6. Set a chain of command where each team member is held accountable for their performance by one primary manager above them.

7. Request that each associate documents their workflows according to standard procedure across your firm, and request that everyone follows said procedure.

5. Acknowledgement

Why is it vital to regularly acknowledge your team members for their efforts and achievements?

If team members aren't regularly acknowledged for their efforts, they will start to feel unappreciated, which will soon cause them to become unresponsive to your requests. Their levels of performance will subsequently fall.

Can you imagine what it's like for an associate to come to work at your firm each day and to feel constant pressure to hit specific targets?

What would it be like if – however hard you work and whatever you achieve – it *never* seems like what you do is enough?

This is how law firm associates, managers, and team members all feel at some point, especially if they don't receive regular appreciation for their efforts.

How long do you think an associate or employee can remain enthusiastic about working at your firm and willing to stay in their position if they don't feel appreciated for their endeavours?

Of course, this is hard to answer. However, it's likely they will break their employment contract with you before it ends, or they'll certainly leave when you don't want them to.

The legal sector is renowned for its high staff turnover, and a major cause of this is exactly what is mapped out above… many associates and employees break their employment contracts early because they don't feel acknowledged enough for their efforts.

The acknowledgement your team members need to feel is mainly facilitated through verbal conversation, but this isn't everything. As I mentioned in the *Team Loyalty* chapter, you will also need to ensure your team members are getting what they want to keep them interested and engaged in their roles. This could be anything from job security and pay rises to learning new skills or advancing along the career track they aspire to.

Achieving these longer-term, personal objectives – as a by-product of their roles in your firm – can, at times, seem far away for them. However, to keep people motivated and engaged in their positions, week-to-week, acknowledging them for their efforts regularly is highly effective.

Why is this, and how can we implement effective recognition at work?

1. Acknowledgement makes team members feel valued, which inspires them to do more for your law firm's success.

One thing we all share as human beings is that we feel good when we notice progress towards some target or ambition that is important to us.

When we're in school, there's nothing like that feeling when we see our exam results, and we've scored the odd A and B (well, it was for me; in my GCSE grades, I initially got an E for maths and an F for geography!).

Joking aside, there's nothing like doing work for someone and being praised for what we have accomplished.

At home, by comparison, we are left with a nice warm feeling when a partner or family member commends us for helping to make the home a better place to be. "Thank you, it looks so nice when it's clean here. I love it." A feeling that we are appreciated manifests inside us, and we feel closer to the person who has acknowledged us. More importantly, it motivates us to do more of what they commended us for.

An example of acknowledgement in your firm is to imagine you've reminded everyone (on a weekly firm-wide meeting or video conference call) that your firm has an agreement that all associates are to hit 100 hours of billing per month.

A month later, you then check the data of one of your departments and see they have improved, but they are still under your firm-wide agreed target.

This may be frustrating to you, but the worst way to approach this is to get into a meeting with that head of department and say, 'You've *still* not got your team to hit their targets. I feel like I have to keep repeating myself over and over again, and yet your team are *still* not doing what they are told.'

The head of department will be left with a feeling that however much effort they've put in, it's resulted in nothing for them. It has only resulted in you pointing out what they've done wrong and how displeased you are.

This is terrible management and leadership because speaking like this to another team member is destructive to their sense of team spirit and morale. It will quickly cause them to feel unappreciated; they will start to pretend they are busy in their role and allow their and their team's performance to dwindle.

If this continues, they'll soon be open to new opportunities at another firm, and you may well lose them before they've truly hit their potential in your company. This might even leave you with a mess to clear up.

Instead, in such a scenario, effective leadership and management would lead you to say something like, 'I've had a look at the recorded billable targets your team hit last month and – out of your team of 12 – you've had four hit the 100-hour target, which is one more than the month before. On average, between the rest of them, they've each billed an extra nine hours compared to the month before. This is a brilliant progress!

'I want you to see how I notice how hard you work, and what an amazing difference you make to all of us here. If you keep going this way, you are going places.'

How good would you feel if your boss spoke to you like this?

Wouldn't you feel like you want more of this and want to continue to put your effort into your role? I know I would!

> " I've learned that people will forget what you said, people will forget what you did, but people will never forget how you made them feel. "
>
> **Maya Angelou**

This is why acknowledging your team members for their achievements and efforts is so effective at inspiring them to continue working hard in their roles. It goes without saying that this is highly likely to keep your firm on track for ever greater success.

After such an acknowledgement you can then say, 'Going forward, what ways can you see to further increase your team's billable hours, so that more in your team hit their 100-hour target?'

Because of the great acknowledgement, your head of department will be much more likely to be open with you, make fresh suggestions, and even implement new solutions to increase their team's billable hours further.

2. Acknowledgments help decrease the number of employees who want to leave your firm.

As I've mentioned, a major cause for law firm employees breaking their employment contract is that they don't feel appreciated or acknowledged enough for their efforts and achievements.

The solution, here, is to acknowledge them *regularly* for the effort they put in, or when they improve their performance in some way.

Naturally, at times, you'll have a team member who – even after several months of effort and regular acknowledgements – doesn't display any particular increase in performance or value to your firm.

In such cases, you need to hold them to account on their agreed targets, and if needs be, point out the agreements they've continually broken. Let them know that unless you see a significant improvement, you'll need to demote them or let them go.

It would be a nice thing if we never had to do this, but the truth is you are running a business, and if a team member – after several months – is not advancing your firm's objectives effectively, you need to be honest with yourself and them about this. If it is necessary to end their employment contract, so be it, you'll cause yourself frustration and inner conflict otherwise.

If you let a lack of performance improvement continue, you are communicating to everyone else in the firm that not working towards fulfilling your firm's objectives is acceptable. This can lead to a firm-wide culture of low performance and bad teamwork.

> "
> Teamwork is the ability to work together toward a common vision. The ability to direct individual accomplishments toward organizational objectives. It is the fuel that allows common people to attain uncommon results.
> "
>
> **Andrew Carnegie**

3. Acknowledgements are one of the most effective ways of elevating your team's performance.

My client, Michael (not his real name), has employees who mainly operate remotely. Some of his departments, however, deliver better work when staff are present in one of his firm's offices because the juniors get more support from the seniors.

Originally, Michael thought little of this variance and dismissed the idea that his employees should have to travel to work a few days in their nearest office. Recently, though, Michael has started to acknowledge his team members regularly as part of his weekly, firm-wide meetings over Zoom, and at one of these recent get-togethers, he acknowledged one team member in particular. This associate had started travelling to work at the office nearest to him for two days per week.

Michael acknowledged this employee for doing so because he usually avoided travelling to work in one of the firm's offices (he nearly always worked from home, instead). With everyone else listening, Michael pointed out how this showed a real commitment to the firm and to being *supportive of his colleagues.*

The week afterwards, Michael was shocked at what he saw happen. With no other requests or prompting, numerous other team members also started to leave their homes a few more days a week and work in their local offices.

Michael was taken aback at this because, in the past, he'd suggested staff work a few more days per week in their nearest office, and this had made no difference. Yet here he was. The acknowledgement of just one team member motivated others to replicate their action.

This is a clear demonstration of how powerful acknowledgements can elevate performance and get team members to do more of what you want.

This isn't manipulation as long as you feel that *what* you acknowledge your team members for is genuinely worthy of acknowledgement (e.g., work done well, work done on time, etc).

For nearly everyone, it is easy to get lost in firefighting at work and have to handle day-to-day pressure. In doing so, we can easily lose sight of our objectives and those of the firm we work for. But when someone stops us and points out what we are doing well, it clarifies what we need to focus on – which keeps us on track.

4. Acknowledgements are effective in writing but are most effective when given verbally.

On some occasions, writing to tell someone how well they are doing can be effective. However, when someone looks us in the eye and tells us – in person – how well we are doing (and *specifically* points out what we are doing well), this impacts us on a much deeper level.

Law firm owners trying to run their firms through email (and excessive numbers of emails, at that!) is a mistake I see all too often. It is more effective to have regular one-on-one and group meetings to make agreements verbally and then document what has been agreed upon afterwards.

Use these meetings to acknowledge team members verbally!

5. Acknowledge regularly, especially before giving corrective instruction.

It's easy to get frustrated with what team members have not accomplished, or agreements they've broken. One skill that's changed my life, however, is learning not to express my frustration right away when I feel let down, but instead to use the frustration I feel as a *cue* to first acknowledge them *before* giving corrective instruction or explaining my side of an argument.

On email, even if someone has emailed back some information or opinion that I find very frustrating, I've learned it's effective for the recipient if I always start with something like, 'Hi John, thanks for taking the time to write this out.'

This applies *even more* when we need to speak to someone we feel has let us down, or not done what we've agreed they would.

When we are frustrated with someone else's behaviour or lack of action, it's especially good to dissipate emotion by taking deep breaths *before* acknowledging them for something they've done well recently or their effort. Then, when we delve into the meeting further, we can take the confrontational sting out of the situation.

You can say something like, 'How are you? I must say, I see the effort you put in around here, and the work you deliver to our firm's clients is great.'

This helps set a good foundation for a good working conversation and makes the team member feel acknowledged for their efforts.

At this stage, they might suspect that they're in trouble or have done something wrong, so this is an ideal time to say something like, 'Before I go on, remember, there's never anything wrong and only ever something missing, and I've seen something that I'd like to point out to you that will improve even further what you do around here.'

This way of speaking to someone puts them at ease and makes them much more receptive to hearing what you want to say next, alongside any corrective instruction you then offer.

Remember to avoid 'advising' where possible. Instead, ask the team member to tell you what caused the lack of the desired result, and ask them what they can do to ensure the same doesn't happen again.

As I've mentioned before, not advising them (i.e., telling them what to do) but instead having them make suggestions is much more effective in preventing the same mistakes from being made.

6. How to effectively acknowledge a team member.

An effective acknowledgement leaves the one being acknowledged with three fundamental standpoints:

1. Feeling respected and valued for their efforts or actions.
2. Able to understand – specifically– what they did well.
3. Able to gain insight as to the level of positive impact their effort or action is having on their colleagues and the firm's clients.

Here is an example of an effective acknowledgement.

'Samatha, I must say how you handled the situation with client X was very good.

'They emailed to tell us about the mistake we made and how some of the files were missing. From what I understand, you then called the client and listened to what they had to say. Later, you spoke to X and X in the team to quickly deliver what was needed for the client.

'Though we made the mistake in the first place, the way you handled this was truly great. You made the client feel valued. Because of how you handled this, we won't lose them, which means you've helped preserve our good reputation, and we'll likely get more work from them.

'Do you get what an amazing team member you are to us all here?'

Such an acknowledgement is effective because it fulfils the three elements of an effective acknowledgement. Samantha will leave the meeting feeling valued, she will know – specifically – what she did well, and she will see the positive impact of her actions on the firm and client.

> **"** Outstanding leaders go out of the way to boost the self-esteem of their personnel. If people believe in themselves, it's amazing what they can accomplish. **"**
>
> **Sam Walton (Founder of Walmart & Sam's Club)**

7. Acknowledgments given in a one-on-one setting versus in a group setting.

One-on-one acknowledgements (as I've detailed above) are very effective at elevating the performance of that one receiver. However, when the same acknowledgement is given to a team member in a group conversation, this has a much wider, positive impact on your firm. As you've read in the example of Michael acknowledging his team member for coming into the office more often, it *inspired* more across the firm to do the same.

This is because people thrive on seeing their status elevated in the eyes of others. In fact, this is often much more motivating than being paid more money.

It makes sense that when we don't enjoy our work, no amount of money makes us better at what we do. Conversely, when we feel we are making a real difference in other's lives, and we are acknowledged for it, it is motivational. It becomes a virtuous circle for carrying out great work and serving those around us.

When a team member hears another member effectively acknowledged, it often sparks a little jealousy in them. They want to receive some of that same credit, and to have their sense of status raised, too.

Because of this, team members who witness commendations are likely to consciously or subconsciously mirror what the acknowledged person did. They will also try to gain some of your praise in the future.

Acknowledgement Revision

1. If you don't ensure your team members feel regularly acknowledged by you or by their manager, they'll likely feel under-appreciated and – because of this – they might end their employment contract early.

2. Acknowledgements make employees even more loyal and help elevate their performances.

3. Acknowledgements are much more effective when given verbally and in group settings.

4. Give acknowledgements regularly and *before* giving corrective instruction in one-on-one calls or as part of firm-wide meetings.

5. To train your team effectively, acknowledge someone for what they did well in a team meeting.

6. Effective acknowledgement leaves the receiver feeling valued for what they've done, gives them specific clarity on what they've done well, and makes them aware of their action's positive impact.

Kate Burt Case Study

In this case study we get to learn how Kate Burt (Solicitor and CEO of HiveRisk) went from working on three laptops at once to growing her team by 12 new members, and delegating away all her fee-earning work and admin while increasing the firm's revenue by 392% in one year.

Kate worked as a solicitor for over 20 years before setting up her own business, helping other law firms and solicitors to be compliant in a highly regulated environment. Her client base spanned sole practitioners to top 10 UK law firms and international law firms.

Initially, Kate was an in-house head of risk and then a consultant on her own, but soon enough, her ambition was to expand what she could offer. She knew she had to start growing a team to bring service to more firms.

Kate had soon built a great name for herself and her compliance services, but she was in a familiar scenario. She was the owner of a firm and a key technician who was very confident in her abilities. This meant she was doing a lot of operational business work and billing work herself.

"I've got photographs I took of myself and how exhausted I was at that time," she said. "I was working in a co-working space at the time, and I would have three laptops on my desk and was literally working on all of them at once."

At the time, Kate worked for several clients and struggled to keep up with demand. Pure grit and determination got Kate this far, but she was at a stage where servicing so many clients wasn't sustainable. Though her clients were happy, Kate was often overworked and exhausted.

At this point, Kate realised – with so much work on the horizon – that she wanted to step up as a leader and business owner. She wanted to build a bigger organisation and increase her skills to manage such growth.

As Kate worked with Dan, one of the initial insights Kate gained (as a business owner) was that it's often assumed she should be the one doing billable technical work. Kate needed to let go of feeling guilty for not doing such work. She needed to feel it was okay and right to delegate this to someone else.

Many law firm owners struggle with this. They assume that their worth to their firms is based on them doing plenty of billable legal work. This isn't true, especially when a firm employs ten or more team members. Kate knew this on a logical level. As a business owner who wanted to increase the number of clients her firm could serve at once (and, in turn, increase her profits), she needed to delegate away her billable work and not be a technician.

"I needed not to feel guilty for not being the someone who's delivering the work all the time. That was a massive shift for me to make."

Kate understood that allowing someone else to do the billable work would enable her to focus effectively on other work, ensuring her clients received an even better level of service and making the firm more profitable.

One of the skills Kate learned (which prevented her from being snowed under with work) was letting go of being the *solution-finder* in her firm.

Kate learned not to tell her team what to do, or how to do it, but rather to question them in a supportive manner and allow them to come up with their own most effective actions and solutions. This is the skill of moving from advisor to leader.

Kate gave her time to support her consultants and empower them to send work directly to clients without her checking it first. Kate saw that it was key to give her consultants the opportunity to be trusted, which removed her from being a bottleneck in the business and its ability to handle much greater volumes of client work.

Another skill Kate learned was how to move clients over to other team members. She did this by introducing the new fee earners to her clients in a timely way. She invited associates who had earned her trust onto three-way calls and meetings with her clients and allowed them to build rapport with each other.

"Our clients work with us because they know us and they trust us. So, we've got to get them to a position where they know, like, and trust the *other* team members. Introducing them in a safe way – where I'm still on the call or in person – and then allowing that team member to say something that's really smart, or say something that's a really good value-add, is key. The client sees them as approachable, but also knowledgeable and authoritative."

Kate makes a great point. Effective delegation isn't about just telling someone what to do and hoping for the best. It's about mentoring the delegate and giving them the opportunity to become trusted by you and your clients before stepping up the level of responsibility given to them.

Kate added, "Once that confidence is in, I could step back from the relationship and allow it to continue with the team member."

Kate also saw that although junior admin members provide a massive amount of value to a firm, they don't take the truly heavy work off a firm owner's shoulders. She found that employing more experienced team members enabled her to build a team to which she could quickly delegate her workload.

A technical director was one of Kate's first employees, who was (and still is) on a significant full-time salary. They were able to take over Kate's heaviest workload directly.

"We did have consultants that I could delegate to, but the employment of a technical director was a really significant turning point for us as a business. He could take over everything, literally everything. There's nothing that I could do that Gavin couldn't do. So that was amazing.

"A lot of business owners try hiring somebody to do virtual assistant work or little bits of admin work here and there, but in the end, they're still facing this mountain of work. That's just overwhelming. And it's only when that gets shifted off their plate that they then have the freedom to start doing all the recruiting, business development, and everything else that goes with it.

"I think that it wouldn't have touched the sides for us to get a VA in, or admin support, even if it was full-time admins and admin support. It wouldn't actually take anything off my plate. It might help me work more efficiently, but in terms of the heavy lifting of the actual work delivery, that wouldn't have helped.

"We're in the process of making some really big decisions right now. And it's exactly that same energy, but on an even bigger scale, which I'm sure will all come together in the weeks to come. It's mentality. One where I think, 'Are we doing this or are we not doing it?' 'Do we go in bigger, or are we going home?' We're gutsy."

After a year of working with me, Kate had grown her team by nine on the payroll and another five consultants.

In terms of the increase in revenue, Kate says, "It went from, like, 70,000 to nearly half a million. It's night and day, really, isn't it? In the last 12 months, I've certainly changed as a person and as a professional."

Nowadays, Kate isn't required to do any of the billable work in her firm; she also has full control over her diary and is able to work the hours she chooses. One of the strategies that made this possible for Kate was to start timetabling herself into her own schedule. She set her schedule so she couldn't be contacted before 11 a.m. and after a certain time at the end of each working day.

"I went to Mallorca last year," she explained. "We had Justine covering operations, Gavin covering all the technical work and – by this point – we'd also hired another analyst as well. And so, actually, everything was completely covered. I didn't have to check in while I was away, and when I got back, it had been plain sailing. They'd won more work and they delivered the work. All the clients were happy. And they'd also done speaking engagements."

With an increase in revenue comes questions about how to spend the money.

"We always reinvest that profit into growing the business. So, the bottom line doesn't look incredible, but we've now got premises, we've got infrastructure, we've got reliable teams in place and everything else.

"The money's coming in, and we're using it in a way that benefits our business, which is on track for greater turnover and profit."

What advice would Kate give to a law firm owner or partner who is overwhelmed with their workload and trying to do a lot of billing work themselves?

"I think when you're in it, it's all consuming; it's so overwhelming.

"You need to visualise a scenario where it's *not* you doing the work all the time. Stepping back, taking some time out to get some perspective, realising that there is another way, and allowing other people in to support you might actually deliver a better service for the client.

"I think, often with solicitors especially, when we're close to the work, we feel like we know best; only we can do the work this well – no one else can. But that's not necessarily the case.

"If we get that perspective and step back and allow others in, not only can they do the work well *as well as* we can, but often they can do it better and more quickly. So, it's having that faith in others and not feeling it's completely all on you.

"The changes have had the greatest impact on the quality of my life. I would say it's the scheduling in time for myself, and not just using that time to run a business. I now have time for myself and other work I enjoy."

So, anybody could just do that? Just start scheduling themselves in?

"Well, they could, but in reality, they won't. I didn't do so until nine months into working with Dan. From the beginning, what also worked well was the weekly calls with team members to ensure that there was sign-off on what they needed to do and that everything was happening. That way, I didn't need to keep contacting them throughout the week.

"We discussed the one-on-one calls with my leadership team as well as delegation. Nothing is actually delegated until the responsibility is transferred. So, you can say, 'Can you do this?' and they can go and do it, but if you've not fully transferred the responsibility, then it's still *on you*. They must feel like they are the person you've delegated it to, and that they have ownership and responsibility.

"Getting good at having difficult conversations was also very useful. Having those really difficult conversations with people, whether that's a team member or a client.

"Sometimes you don't know whether it's your communication that's missing or somebody's participation that's missing. But, once you know that your leadership and management delivers clear requests, accountability, not advising but leading, and all those other things, things will work out in the end."

After speaking to Kate's financial director, it was confirmed that after one year of working with Dan, her firm – HiveRisk – had seen a 392% increase in revenue compared to the year before. At the same time, Kate became totally free of technical, billable work, which now gives her lots of free time to work on building her business, the work she enjoys, and what is most impactful for her business.

> "
> Change will not come if we wait for some other person or some other time. We are the ones we've been waiting for. We are the change that we seek.
> "
>
> **Barack Obama**

What Now?

So, here you are… one of those particularly disciplined law firm owners who has read to the end of this book. Now what?

We've covered a lot of information here and, because of this, it's likely difficult to know where to start. As such, I wanted to break down some steps for you to take going forward.

I suggest you only move on to each next step after you have implemented the previous one. At a minimum, this should be to a point where the implementation of the previous step is manageable for you as you proceed.

If you follow these steps and implement each one, I assure you that you will soon see rewarding results. If done well, you will also see an increase in the profitability of your firm while reducing your workload.

1. For any equity member, colleague, or associate you have an unresolved dispute with, or who you've treated badly in the past in some way, arrange a one-on-one meeting or phone call with them. In this meeting, take responsibility for what you've done or how you've treated them and just say sorry. Then, make a promise that – going forward – you won't ever do that again to them or anyone else. This will likely require a huge level of courage, but you will be astounded by the freedom and ease this will bring to your life, and how much this will increase your ability to lead and manage your team members effectively. If your dispute concerns remuneration or something too complex, reach out to an expert with experience of guiding law firm executives to solve such issues. There are often other solutions. Whatever you do, don't try implementing everything covered in this book on top of broken relationships because they simply will not be effective.

2. If you don't already have such a policy in place, make an announcement – at your next firm-wide meeting – that gossiping, judging, and discrimination of any sort will no longer be tolerated at your firm. Explain how harmful and destructive such communication is to creating a work environment that feels safe for everyone and which

thrives. Then, ensure everyone across the firm is clear about trying to first solve any problems directly with whomever they concern. After that, check that everyone is clear on the chain of command and that everyone has someone they feel they can openly talk to (who they report to) should they have any problems. Explain that if they can't solve it with them, they are to take it to the person in the chain of command above them, and to continue escalating their problem this way until it's resolved.

3. Schedule regular, weekly, one-on-one in-person or video call meetings with each of your heads of department or – if in a smaller firm – with each of your employees. Either way, no more than 10 team members who report to you at once.

4. In these one-on-one meetings, firstly get clear on what each head of department, manager, or associate wants to succeed at, both in and out of their role in your firm.

5. Create a document (ideally online) that you can both access. When together, write down their personal and business targets.

6. Break down those targets into quarterly targets with the team member, and distinguish – *together* – the most effective actions that the team member needs to do to achieve them. Write them down.

7. Practise making clear requests of your colleagues. This includes requesting others to do things with clear instructions of exactly what the request is and a time frame by when it needs to be completed. Get your colleagues to confirm what has just been agreed, then document it on their weekly call tracking document.

8. To avoid being manipulative, always be willing to give anyone you manage the choice to either accept, decline, or counteroffer any request you make of them.

9. Choose to never speak to anyone in an angry or frustrated tone again. Make a commitment to be someone who anyone in your team can fully express their thoughts with.

10. In the following weeks' one-on-one calls, check to see if team members have done what they promised they would do. For the things

they haven't, guide them to discover why they haven't done what they said they would do. Guide them to think of and implement a solution to each going forwards.

11. Make these one-on-one calls non-negotiable and keep them to one per week. If there isn't enough to cover on each call, make them shorter. If needed, even a 15-minute call per week is all that's needed to hold a high-performing associate to account.

12. Set a chain of command map so that everyone in your firm has one other person they are accountable to. Then, ensure that everyone across your firm has a weekly one-on-one meeting (in-person or on video) with the person they are accountable to. This meeting is to make sure they are clear on their targets and supported to best meet them.

13. Set a weekly firm-wide in-person or video conference meeting. In these calls, ensure the meetings always start with fun banter. Then, always acknowledge someone for something they've done well; something that you want to see happen more often in your firm. Also, use these firm-wide meetings to share announcements as this will make everyone in the firm feel included and part of something.

14. Calculate the difference in the profitability of your firm between you carrying out one hour of billable work at your charge-out rate versus a team of 10 middleweight associates, each billing an hour at their charge-out rates. If you do this correctly, you'll see it's more profitable for your firm and you if you ensure that all the associates in your firm hit their billing targets rather than focusing on doing more billable work yourself. With this in mind, start delegating your client workload to your firm's more senior members.

Do this gradually, especially with clients you've worked with for a long time, by having firm members involved in three-way meetings or video calls and participating in giving suggestions. Over time, your clients will gain confidence in their abilities, and colleagues can start to effectively take work off your hands, even from those clients you've personally done work for over many years. Use the time that becomes available to support the senior members and ensure they are providing your clients with a great level of service. Once that is happening, reliably focus on business development to create new clients that will have their work done by your senior associates (not you) from the start. Doing so will remove you from being the bottleneck in your firm's profitability, and such actions will even further increase your firm's and your profit while giving you more space to do the work you enjoy.

15. To ensure your managers or heads of department have enough time to support each of the associates they manage to hit their billing targets, set each of them reduced targets, ideally needing to fulfil no more than 50 billable hours per month, as this will give them lots of free time to solve extra challenges in their team's performance as they arise. This will ensure that all your associates hit their billing targets, which – if you've calculated things correctly – you'll see is the most profitable model for your firm and your workload reduction.

16. Start to track everything you do with your time. Practise this for a month, and by the end, you will have a list of all the tasks you do. Look at your list and see what you can delegate next – especially your billable work and the work you no longer enjoy. Then, use the one-on-one calls with each associate or manager who reports to you to clearly request that they take that work off your hands. Then, week by week, on their one-on-one call, provide the support they need to ensure they succeed while also holding them accountable!

17. Whether value-based units or billable hours, set clear, firm-wide billing targets. If you already have these and your associates are reliably hitting them, stick with them. If not (and they are too high), lower them to ideally 100 hours per month for each associate. This number can be very lucrative for you while easily manageable for everyone else. Have your targets announced every week in a firm-wide meeting, then check each manager or head of department is effectively holding the associates that report to them accountable to meet their billing targets.

18. Start to regularly and vocally acknowledge your team members in their weekly one-on-one calls with you, and others on the weekly firm-wide in-person or video meetings. Once these firm-wide meetings become well attended and regular, they can be led by senior members of

your firm and you can be there to listen, support, provide suggestions, and make announcements when needed.

19. Going forward, whenever you find yourself unclear, stuck, or facing a challenge you can't move through, get into communication with someone, anyone. One thing I learned in all my advanced leadership and management training is that anything – absolutely anything – from the smallest annoyance to the greatest problem, can be solved through communication. If you can't think of anyone to talk to because what you face seems so complex or feels so overwhelming, then write to me, and either I can help or I can refer you to someone who can. All communications, as such, are kept strictly confidential. Whatever you do, don't battle alone and suffer; life is far too short, and you have all the support you need; it's just one email or call away.

A New Future

(again)

If you've been left inspired by what you've read in this book, and want to continue gaining useful insights to elevate your management and leadership skills, gain clarity, continually increase your profitability, and build a firm you love working on, then you are welcome to join The Law Firm Owners Club.

It's free, and as a member of this club, you'll get:

- A short email every other week with a core insight that you can implement right away to build an ever-more thriving and satisfying law firm.

- Free tickets to networking events I'll be speaking at; events where you will also gain further insights from other industry leaders.

- The opportunity to meet other law firm owners to share strategies to further speed up your profitability, reduce your heavy workload, gain free time, and do more of the work you enjoy.

If you'd like this or would like to find out more about possibly working with Dan, go to:

www.danwarburton.com

Or scan this QR code:

Other Books from the Publisher

Ditch The Billable Hour! Implementing Value-Based Pricing in a Law Firm

Is the billable hour on its way out? Does *any* client like paying for legal services by the hour?

With generative artificial intelligence soon to create tidal waves in the legal industry – helping lawyers to create legal documents in mere seconds – the time-honoured billable hour is under threat more than ever. But what is the alternative?

In *Ditch The Billable Hour!,* Shaun Jardine explains how lawyers should move away from *time* as the driving element of pricing, and focus on the results that clients want to achieve. In doing so, he shows why legal firms need to adopt Value-Based Pricing (VBP), and how to do so.

Ditch The Billable Hour! is the extensive and practical new book, from a former law firm CEO, that is filled with real-world expertise, advice, and perspectives, and which digs deep into all aspects of VBP for the legal industry.

In the book, you will discover

> What clients truly value, and how to have conversations to establish the value that lawyers create.

> How to price and capture a share of that value, and how to create pricing options which give clients choice.

> How to lead and implement the change to make Value-Based Pricing a reality.

> Includes more than 20 interviews with lawyers and other professionals who have views on VBP.

> Includes additional learning resources, hints, tips, and practical exercises, plus a RACI checklist.

Togetherness: How to Build a Winning Team

Togetherness is a powerful state of connection between individuals that can lead to amazing triumphs. If you want the individuals on *your* team to develop their skills and reach their potential, get them 'together'. The key to this, is to understand your players' group memberships and how to harness them, to create a unique team identity that is special to "*us*".

This concise and practical book – from Dr. Matt Slater, a world authority on togetherness – shows you how you can develop togetherness in your team. The journey starts with an understanding of what underpins togetherness and how it can drive high performance and well-being simultaneously. It then moves onto practical tips and activities based on the 3R model (Reflect, Represent, Realise) that you can learn and complete with your team to unlock their *togetherness*.

The 3R model provides you with a framework to take your team on a journey from "*me*" to "*we*".

With memorable stories from the world of high-performance sport, and a robust evidence-base, this book will help you to create and maintain togetherness in your team – whether in sport or other fields such as business or voluntary sectors – simply and effectively.

Achieve the impossible with your team… through togetherness.

(Out)Law: From Teenage Mum to Legal Trailblazer

(Out)Law is a powerful and inspiring journey of survival and resourcefulness, exploring the remarkable life of Alice Stephenson, who defied adversity to become a beacon of change in the legal world. At just 18, Alice faced the challenges of teenage motherhood and homelessness, yet refused to be defined by her circumstances. Determined and focused, she embarked on a path of education, navigating the complexities of university while juggling her responsibilities as a young mother.

Having qualified as a solicitor, Alice had proven that barriers could be broken down thanks to grit and passion, but her story doesn't stop there. In 2017, she set out to disrupt the legal industry by founding her own law firm – Stephenson Law.

(Out)Law is a testament to one person's defiance of societal expectations when coupled with drive and ambition. This book explores the struggles and challenges that women and those whose faces don't fit the mould encounter, as Alice stands against the norms of a male-dominated, elitist legal profession.

Through her journey, Alice not only reshapes the legal landscape but also redefines what it means to be an outlaw – a rebel fighting for justice and change. Taking aim at archaic traditions, outdated perspectives, and an industry rife with discrimination, *(Out)Law* explores how innovation, inclusivity and the humanisation of lawyers are the key to delivering change within one of the world's oldest professions. And, oh yes, how tattoos won't bring the skies crashing onto our heads, either.

(Out)Law is the must-read story of one woman's remarkable journey from teenage mum to legal trailblazer.

You Will Thrive: The Life-Affirming Way to Work and Become What You Really Desire

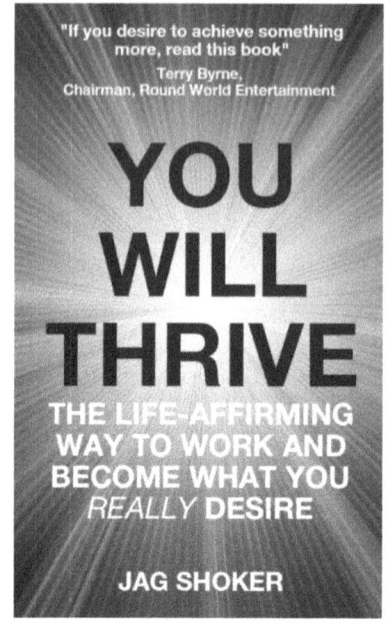

YOU WILL THRIVE

THE LIFE-AFFIRMING WAY TO WORK AND BECOME WHAT YOU *REALLY* DESIRE

JAG SHOKER

Have you lost your spark or the passion for what you do? Is your heart no longer in your work or (like so many people) are you simply disillusioned by the frantic race to get ahead in life? Your sense of unease may be getting harder to ignore, and comes from the growing urge to step off the treadmill and pursue a more thrilling and meaningful direction in life.

You Will Thrive addresses the subject of modern disillusionment. It is essential reading for people looking to make the most of their talents and be something more in life. Something that matters. Something that makes a difference in the world.

Through six empowering steps, it reveals 'the Way' to boldly follow your heart as it leads you to the perfect opportunities you seek. Through every step, it urges you to put a compelling thought to the test:

You possess the power within you to attract the right people, opportunities, and circumstances that you need to become what you desire.

As you'll discover, if you find the faith to act on this power and do the Work required to realise your dream, a testing yet life-affirming path will unfold before you as life orchestrates the Way to make it all happen.

www.ingramcontent.com/pod-product-compliance
Ingram Content Group UK Ltd.
Pitfield, Milton Keynes, MK11 3LW, UK
UKHW050834231224
452744UK00004B/21